Black Gay Man

SEXUAL CULTURES: New Directions from the Center for Lesbian and Gay Studies

General Editors: José Esteban Muñoz and Ann Pellegrini

Times Square Red, Times Square Blue
Samuel R. Delany

Private Affairs
Critical Ventures in the Culture of Social Relations
Phillip Brian Harper

In Your Face
9 Sexual Studies
Mandy Merck

Tropics of Desire
Interventions from Queer Latino America
José Quiroga

Murdering Masculinities
Fantasies of Gender and Violence in the American Crime Novel
Greg Forter

Our Monica, Ourselves

The Clinton Affair and the National Interest

Edited by Lauren Berlant and Lisa Duggan

Black Gay Man

Essays

Robert F. Reid-Pharr, Foreword by Samuel R. Delany

Black Gay Man

Essays

ROBERT F. REID-PHARR

Foreword by Samuel R. Delany

NEW YORK UNIVERSITY PRESS

New York and London

NEW YORK UNIVERSITY PRESS
New York and London

Library of Congress Cataloging-in-Publication Data
Reid-Pharr, Robert, 1965–
Black gay man : essays / Robert Reid-Pharr ; foreword by
Samuel R. Delany.
p.   cm. — (Sexual cultures)
Includes index.
ISBN 0-8147-7502-0 (cloth) — ISBN 0-8147-7503-9 (paper)
1. African American gays. 2. African Americans—Race identity.
3. African Americans—Intellectual life.   I. Title. II. Series.
HQ76.2.U5 R45 2001
305.38'96642—dc21   2001000080

New York University Press books are printed on acid-free paper, and
their binding materials are chosen for strength and durability.

Manufactured in the United States of America

10 9 8 7 6 5 4 3 2 1

Contents

Acknowledgments

For opening innumerable doors for me, to the heart, to the head, to the tools of my trade many thanks and much love go to Lee Baker, Mia Bay, Roberto Bedoya, Jodi Benjamin, Herman Bennett, Antoinette Burton, Hazel Carby, Bill Cohen, Arnaldo Cruz-Malave, Patricia Dixon, Cheryl Dunye, Shelly Eversley, Gerard Fergerson, Carl Fraley, Shari Frilot, Robert Garland, Venita George, Paul Gilroy, Alan Grossman, Siba Grovogui, John Guillory, Phillip Brian Harper, Benjamin Herman, Francisco Herrera, K. Brent Hill, Michael Johnson, Alexandra Juhasz, John Keene, Katrina Bell McDonald, Dwight McBride, Alfred Manuel, Frank Mitchell, Elena Mòdol, Darrell Moore, Jennifer Morgan, Zachary Morgan, Bruce Morrow, José Muñoz, Odena Neale, Eve Oishi, Ricardo Ortiz, John Plotz, Sabiyha Prince, Yevette Richards, Colin Robinson, Joaquim Rodríguez, Joan Saez, Roger Schulte, Robert Sciasi, Eve Sedgwick, Barbara Smith, Paul Smith, Dina Suggs, Ibrahim, Sundiata, Peter Taylor, Sasha Torres, Scott Trafton, Michelle Wallace, Joe Wittreich, Tony Young, and Eric Zinner.

Foreword

Samuel R. Delany

Between the glorious promise of 1848's *Communist Manifesto* and the more focused analysis of 1851's *Eighteenth Brumaire of Louis Bonaparte* (and its darker twin, *The Class Struggle in France: 1848 to 1850*), a problematic intrudes itself into Marx's thought that will trouble the left up to the present day. From the Revolution of 1848 and its fallout over '49, '50, and '51, the thorn in the side of Marx in particular and socialists in general was and has been: Why, in a democratic nation, does the working class—and specifically the most oppressed and exploited segments of the working class—tend to vote in such a politically conservative manner?

Are they deluded? Are they just stupid? Have they been intellectually manipulated? Transfer this question to the black American underclass and its recently emergent middle class—with our histories of massive enslavement and free-issue blacks, of oppression and resistence, of Jim Crow, segregation and black nationalism, our integrationalists and assimilationists, our separatists and Afro-centrists, our melaninists and our culturalists—and it re-complicates into a truly nightmarish theoretical tortuosity.

The fundamental explanation for working class conservatism is, nevertheless, simple and basic—though I am unaware of any place in which Marx formulated it as a clear political principle. The grounding political fact, however, any 18-year-old sweep-up boy with an 80 IQ can probably formulate a version of for himself: "In a money economy, where all my salary comes from X, it is lunatic for *me* to vote against X's best interests."

It does not take a lot to realize that if your boss suffers economically, then everything from your working conditions to your take-home pay is threatened. As a political principle, then, this works as the great stabilizer for democratic money economies. As social progress has come about in the interstices this principle allows for, we have moved toward our current position—the best of all possible worlds? By no means. Still, it is a world that is stable enough that a radically interrogating superstructure can take as its motto and first principle "freedom of speech." And we must remember that it is only those workers—usually urban artisans (a realization Marx did come to)—whose money comes from several social class sources, up and down the social ladder, who can afford to entertain a truly radical political practice.

A second awareness slowly becoming part of leftist thought is simply that, if we believe that a relatively peaceful revolution is preferable to an armed one always to come, then we are—always—within the center, as we are always at the beginning, of that revolution *now*. The stabilizing force of the working class's political conservatism allows that revolution to progress *without* breaking out into armed encounters.

The introduction and nine essays that follow are from a young critic for whom such an awareness as I speak of above is now a stronger—now a weaker—current in his thought. An awareness of the infrastructural stability underlying the superstructural arena in which political debate takes place frees a critic such as Robert F. Reid-Pharr to breech areas of the "the outrageous" with often memorable effect.

I don't agree with all he says. Reid-Pharr thinks that the anti-Semitic rhetoric and ideas here and there associated with black nationalism and the Black Muslim movement (among the most troubling aspects of black working class conservatism) are an expression of black American alienation, where I would say they compensate for that alienation, rather, in a field where anti-Semitic rhetoric has always already been available, so that, through a process akin to Freudian transference, the discourse in which that rhetoric is caught up reproduces an ugly, divisive, and destructive situation. Anti-Semitism from the oppressed represses much, but it expresses little except a hostility that could be a positive energy turned elsewhere. That Reid-Pharr takes on such a topic in a field of such "scandalous" or "outrageous" objectivity is nevertheless to be commended. We must listen to his arguments carefully: there is nothing slapdash or careless about them.

In these pieces we find fascinatingly oblique takes on the image of the "black family," and on Louis Farrakan's controversial "Million Man March" (Reid-Pharr actually went), and on the sadomasochistic images gay black writer Gary Fisher used as parameters around which to organize his fantasies and sexual encounters with some of his sexual partners, before his death from AIDS complications at age 32 in 1993. In Reid-Pharr's notes on Fisher, again we are within the "outrageous," where what is most uncomfortable for us is still the scandalous detachment with which the texts are teased apart. Here is a critic whose radical enterprise is not so much to change your mind about concepts you've already reached a conclusion on. Rather it is to remap the territories of what can and cannot be thought about at all. That he does this in such an engaging and readable style (Have I said? Often these pieces are deliciously funny.) is amazing.

I return a moment to the larger context in which the freshness, the refinement, and the precision of Reid-Pharr's thought resonate. The work of scholars like Philippe Ariès, done back in the fifties and published and translated in the sixties, showed that "the family" was not an institution with its origins in poverty. On the contrary, the family is specifically a bourgeois institution that originates in the upper middle class. In good economic times, it reaches down through various social strata precisely by means of the desire of those below to imitate those better off. When times are bad, it crumbles from the bottom up. (The "family" is, after all, an institution to organize money, food, shelter, culture, language, sexuality, and care—and provides one possible location within which reproduction may take place.) This view serves as a needed corrective to that of the family as a transcultural absolute, arcadian in origin, a given from the lowest to the highest level— an "authentic" form of sociality that is somehow battered and undermined by "inauthentic" forces of urbanism, industrialism, and modernism. The fact is, the family *never* extended down to the lowest levels of society, European or American; the materials which constitute it—money, time, and certain economies of stability, physical and psychological—are simply not available there. And at numerous locations, the lowest social strata of American society are, of course, black.

I bring this up because Reid-Pharr's earlier extraordinary and necessary book, *Conjugal Union: The Body, the House, and the Black American,* his study of four antebellum black American nonfiction [largely] writers—David Walker, Maria Stewart, Henry Bibb, and Frederick Douglass—and four antebellum black American novels—William Wells Brown's *Clotel* [1853], Harriet E. Wilson's *Our Nig* [1859], Frank J. Webb's *The Garies and Their Friends* [1857], and Martin R. Delany's *Blake, or the Huts of America* [1861–62]), takes its lead "from Engel's genealogy of domesticity in which he suggests that, though families are primary locations for the domination and exploitation of women, it is none the less women themselves who produce familiar structures in order to establish bulwarks against harsher, unsentimental forms of male domination, slavery chief among them" (CJ 6). Without Ariès's rigorously materialist critique, however, it is almost impossible not to start "blaming the victims" of family structure, as even Engels starts to do as his "family" slips into that transcultural/transcendent image. It is a critique that lends its intelligence to Reid-Pharr's analysis of the black family as a structure of images and desires.

Within his chosen texts, Reid-Pharr astutely untangles the markings of difference (to achieve and mark power, autonomy, even menace) from the equally necessary disavowal/disallowance of difference (to achieve and mark parity, equality, even peace), an oscillation that may be taken as a fundamental structure of racialized discourse itself. While the essays in *Black Gay Man* refuse aloofness with the same gesture that they refuse to be intimidated by identity politics, *Conjugal Union* is a dense, patient book that deftly interrogates "the black self" and "the black community," as it undertakes to "unpack the common sense of that deep tendency within black intellectual life to insist upon black singularity, to conjure that which is pure, unique, that which is decidedly black." Yet for all their differences in style, both books negotiate a single set of assumptions.

To understand those assumptions, one must ask, what indeed is the purpose of black singularity, this "pure," this "unique," this authentic blackness, that is to say this cascade of essentialist rhetoric with which black intellectual life in America has been marked from its beginnings. Is it simply an attempt to transcendentalize the notion of race itself to keep its God-given authority in place? One explanation of course is that we use different vocabularies in different situations, at different degrees of formality. People still use geocentric rhetoric such as "sunrise" and "sunset" who are quite aware of—and wholly in concurrence with—the heliocentric vision of the solar system. But the abuses of essentialism are much closer to us than the abuses of the Inquisition—and thus those of us who are aware of them are also likely to be more wary. I suspect, however, the valid aspect of so much black critical energy trying to redeem this rhetoric of late is, rather, an attempt to *ethnicize* black life—because the one notion that is most undercut by the concept of "race" is the concept of an *ethnos*, a *nationhood*. The problematic here, however, is that there is no nation, no ethnos that doesn't turn on a theory internal to it *of* ethnic transcendence, i.e., an ethnic essence. Thus Reid-Pharr's enterprise is to insist that the effect of authentic blackness, whether from a nation or an ethnos, "exists within history and [is] thus permeable and dynamic" (CJ 6). In short, however "absolute" it looks at any given historical moment, it is still a social construct and changes with time. Side by side with this goes the attempt to deconstruct, if you will, the self-evident notion that "Black American culture emanates from Black American bodies," through a patient reading not of some intrusive, polluting, either dominating *or* inauthentic white cultural elements, but rather of black texts, and black texts from before the confusions of emancipation and reconstruction recomplicated and syncopated the logic of racialist discourse into what is now generally spoken of as "racism." The argument of that earlier work is one with the rhetorical drama played out across the more playful surface of the more recent essays here: What constitutes an authentic black body—and therefore what constitutes the black culture it might produce—has been contested since (and well before) the foundations of the United States of America and its fundamental and founding Hellenic contradiction of a democratic nation resting (so uneasily) on a slave economy.

Such an intellectual performance as Robert F. Reid-Pharr's requires that the arguments be careful and historically astute. In turn, this means, for the reader, that the urge to foreclose them before they are as carefully read and evaluated must be patiently resisted. (Quite honestly, it took me two slow and lingering readings of *Conjugal Union* to realize what an extraordinary book it is—whereas I had read the essays in *this* book through three times almost before I realized it.) Robert F. Reid-Pharr's work is as important for an understanding of the motile and protean trajectories of racialized concepts around and throughout the old rhetorical parameters of what race means (and might mean) in America as is Judith Butler's work on the equally beleaguered topic of gender. It will repay your attentive reading with a range of writerly pleasures on many levels.

It is an honor to recommend it.

Works Cited

Ariès, Philippe. Translated by Robert Baldick. *Centuries of Childhood: A Social History of Family Life.* (A translation of *L'Enfant et la vie familiale sous l'ancien regime,* ©1960 by Librarie Plon, Paris.) New York: Vintage Books, 1962.

Brown, William Wells. *Clotel, or, The President's Daughter.* 1853. Reprint. New York: University Books, 1969.

Delany, Martin R. Edited by Floyd J. Miller. *Blake, or, The Huts of America.* 1861–62. Reprint. Boston: Beacon Press, 1970.

Engels, Frederick. *The Origin of the Family, Private Property and the State in Light of the Researches of Lewis H. Morgan.* 1884. Reprint. New York: International Publishers, 1942.

Fisher, Gary. Edited and with an afterword by Eve Kosofsky Sedgwick. *Gary in Your Pocket: Stories and Notebooks of Gary Fisher.* Durham: Duke University Press, 1996.

Marx, Karl. Edited by Frederic L. Bender. *The Class Struggle in France: 1848 to 1850.* 1850. Reprint. New York: International Publishers Co., 1964.

———. *The Communist Manifesto.* 1848. Reprint. A Norton Critical Edition. New York: W. W. Norton, 1988.

———. *The Eighteenth Brumaire of Louis Bonaparte.* 1852. Reprint. New York: International Publishers Co., 1962.

Reid-Pharr, Robert F. *Conjugal Union: The Body, the House and the Black American.* New York: Oxford University Press, 1999.

Webb, Frank J. Introduction by Robert F. Reid-Pharr. *The Garies and Their Friends.* 1857. Reprint. Baltimore: Johns Hopkins University Press, 1997.

Wilson, Harriet E. *Our Nig; or, Sketches from the Life of a Free Black, in a Two-Story White House, North.* 1859. Reprint. New York: Random House, 1983.

Introduction

Perhaps the most difficult aspect of completing this collection has been coming to terms with the work's title, *Black Gay Man*. The reason for my difficulty is not only the rather obvious fact that one's identity cannot possibly be summed up by the phrase or any of its derivatives—Negro queer, colored sissy, nigger faggot—but also that every time I hear the designation, I feel almost as if I am somehow denying a basic reality of my intellectual temperament. Much of my work, much of the work included within this collection, has been straightforwardly designed to help dismantle the American identity machine, to break its hold on the collective imagination. Yet, strangely, I find that, like many of my peers, I continuously use the mechanisms of that machine to affect its dysfunction. One should remember that the articulation of multiple identities was—and is—thought to be a corrective to outmoded binaristic identitarian discourses: black/white, gay/

straight, man/woman. This tendency led some of the nation's most talented intellectuals to feast at the banquet table of queer theory where one was assured that identity was not simply diffuse and diverse but constructed, unstable, and performative, as well.

I have long been skeptical, however, of the political and social efficacy of this line of thought outside the more rarefied precincts of academia. Indeed, I have become increasingly alarmed by the fact that, although remarkable strides have been made within queer theory and other recent theoretical trends with regard to what I will call the disarticulation of identity, there seems to have been precious little movement forward in our understanding of how to affect basic economic and social structures. We continue to exist in a country in which the most assertive and cogent articulations of the problems and possibilities inherent within American life seem to come most often from the right, or from so-called centrists bent on appeasing more sober elements of the right. Meanwhile, left intellectuals seem at times more concerned with demonizing one another or engaging in ever more obtuse forms of theoretical posturing than with speaking to the everyday concerns of our people and our nation.

This is not at all to imply that I have remained aloof from the theoretical movements that I have witnessed over the past two decades, movements that have demonstrably altered the manner in which much work within a variety of disciplines gets done. Still, I must confess that the seeming lack of interest in producing work that concretely affects the lives of American people makes it difficult for me to believe that we have changed—or challenged—basic structures of race, gender, class, and sexuality. The disarticulation of identity comes at precisely the moment when many American institutions, particularly American universities, are less and less hospitable to poor people, Black American people, and other people of color. Indeed, some of the most successful attacks on affirmative action have taken place within the same locations that nurtured the emergent notions of identity by which many of us—myself included—have been beguiled.

I am not asking that we return to notions of strategic essentialism, or any mode of essentialism for that matter. On the contrary, I am as weary of carrying around banal ideas about human difference as almost anyone else. At the same time, I find in rereading these essays that in each of them I am groping for a method by which to bridge the divide between theory and practice, to break down barriers between the ways in which I think about American life as a professional critic and the manner in which I comport myself in my everyday passings. Thus, this collection represents part of my struggle to make sense of a world in which it seems the tired horse of identity politics desperately needs to be withdrawn but in which nonetheless few workable options for the production of a progressive political discourse seem to be in the offing. In the world in which I live and write there are extremely cohesive and active black, gay, lesbian, feminist, and labor movements. There is not a cohesive community of American progressives with, say, national organizations, recognized and respected leaders, clearly defined agendas, a well-developed intellectual class, and a broad-based grass-roots constituency. There is not a fully empowered national political party that might rightly be labeled leftist. In fact, I cannot recall any time in my life when a community of progressives, a community with an identity distinct from that of any of its constituent elements, actually existed, although there have been consistent calls by intellectuals for a return to the notion of an American progressivism apart from the identity politics that are now so easy to bemoan. And yet, we seem never to get back to the place from which, presumably, we started.

Scholars like Richard Rorty, John Patrick Diggins, and Russell Jacoby continually bemoan the loss of a coherent community of left activists and intellectuals. And, while I have sympathy for the arguments of these intellectuals and the many others whom they represent, I continue to be somewhat stunned by the sense within their writing that the American left faces more danger from the ranks of feminists, gay activists, and Afrocentrists than it does from the self-proclaimed conservatives against whom these communities are often the first line of defense. Rorty writes:

Leftists in the academy have permitted cultural politics to supplant real politics, and have collaborated with the Right in making cultural issues central to public debate. They are spending energy which should be directed at proposing new laws on discussing topics as remote from the country's needs as were Adams' musings on the Virgin and the Dynamo. The academic Left has no projects to propose to America, no vision of a country to be achieved by building a consensus on the need for specific reforms. Its members no longer feel the force of James's and Croly's rhetoric. The American civic religion seems to them narrow-minded and obsolete nationalism.[1]

The name calling here, the insistence that those on the left interested in matters of culture not only have been thrown off balance by rightist elements within the nation but indeed have been in active collusion with them, turns precisely on Rorty's refusal to give up on the idea of a singular American identity brought into focus by the great and good wars of the mid-twentieth century. He continues to hold up the bloody shirt of a disempowered, soft, ineffectual left, not because of the looming threat of evil empires concocting diabolical plans to disrupt the American way of life but instead because of a nostalgia for a world in which one might actually articulate an American life, an American mission, an American promise.

It is in this sense that I, like many others, find Rorty at once maddening and compelling. On the one hand, his image of a left steeped in the lyrical Americanism of William James and Herbert Croly necessarily elicits the ugly historical critique that Rorty clumsily avoids. It is frankly doubtful that the intensity of James's prose or the clarity of Croly's logic did more to affect the dismantling of, say, formal structures of segregation than did the self-consciously culturalist machinations of an Elaine Brown, a Huey Newton, or a Robert Williams. At the same time, it is certain not only that the mass political and cultural movements of the last part of the twentieth century produced avenues by which a variety of leftists came into academic life but that these movements sustain the very ground on which Rorty—and I—offer our critique. My fear is that Rorty comes dangerously close to the unsavory assumption that not only must we resuscitate the gospel of America but that in the process the priests of the American church must necessarily remain aloof from the ideological and cultural structures by which the American citizenry makes sense of its environment.

Still, it is not easy to discard Rorty, not easy to discount the singularity of his call for an American progressivism, not easy to dismiss his dream for a just, peaceful, and prosperous nation. I suggest that where Rorty fails is not in his thirst for a new Americanism but in his distrust for not only the much maligned left academy but also the everyday realities of American progressive life. The admittedly contradictory nature of American left politics, the emphasis on identities that Rorty finds so distasteful, is as American, one must remember, as any appeals to the essentially transcendent nature of American identity. I argue, in fact, that Rorty misses the point that the American philosophers whom he celebrates—James, Dewey, Croly, Whitman, Lincoln—were able to produce their utopian images of the nation not in spite of the incredible differences that they witnessed but, on the contrary, because of them. There is no way to arrive at the beloved community except through the sullied byways we have produced ourselves, no way to achieve utopia without getting one's hands dirty.

I ask that we begin to rethink our preoccupation with the issue of identity politics and the multitude of sins that, presumably, it engendered. The attack on identitarian discourses is indeed an attack on the actual lived reality of the American left, with all of its many contradictions and confusions. Indeed, embedded within the often sound theoretical critique of various articulations of the self, one often finds embarrassment at the fact that the American left, including American labor, does not engage nearly so often as its European counterparts in Marxist and other forms of universalist discourses to articulate either its theoretical methods or practical modes. It is still very much in vogue for academics to attack each other on the grounds that we have all somehow completely given up on class struggle for the "indulgent" projects of identity and culture. Never mind that there is clearly as much activity in the American populace, inside and outside the academy, around issues of identity, rights, fairness, and inclusion as there is around labor and class. We still have not quite rid ourselves of the fear that the presumed excesses of the sixties, the "petty" cultural politics, "the will to pleasure," the desire to announce one's peculiarity, were indeed so decadent that they need to be met by a seriousness and rigor that often come in the form of barely penetrable prose and theoretical postures that treat American cultural and political life as some great and ugly spectacle of false consciousness.

I believe that the time is ripe for us to be done with the endless hand wringing, the flagellation, the painful—and hermetic—self reflection that has typified much of our work. Instead, I suggest that we begin to celebrate the incredible advances that American progressives, in all our multiplicity, have made in this country and elsewhere. Rorty is right. It is time for us to begin again the challenging labor of articulating, without shame—if not without doubt—a positive vision of the American community, the American tomorrow. As intellectuals, we must refuse once and for all the notion that we exist in a vacuum in which our ideas never seem to escape to the outside world. We must believe that the life of the politically and culturally engaged scholar, activist, teacher, politician, or artist is not simply noble and efficacious but enjoyable. The art and literature of the twenties and thirties, the fashion and politics of the sixties and seventies, the door-by-door, shop-by-shop organizing of labor throughout the two preceding centuries, were all undertaken by people who thought that what they were doing not only was correct but indeed might bring joy into their lives.

When we raise the specter of identity politics, when we offer a stale "no" to political and cultural activism that not only has helped strengthen democracy in America but has also helped people survive and thrive in spite of the horror of American racism, homophobia, class exploitation, anti-intellectualism, militarism, anticommunism, and hard-boiled capitalism, we must at the very least offer an alternative that speaks to the realities of people's lives, the means by which they seek not only for justice but also for beauty, light, the transcendent, the metaphysical. It is futile for those of us who care to aid in the production and reproduction of a progressive community to continue the false distinction between putatively scientific method and our need to produce images of community in which all of us might find some discrete sense of dignity, of self.

I am inspired, in this regard, by the recent work of Slavoj Žižek, who suggests that we not continue the false assumption of a clear distinction between the universal and the particular. Instead, he argues that the universal subject may indeed be she who is clearly left out of narratives of normative (American) life. The black lesbian mother is able to represent clearly the reality and the promise of America because she most often demonstrates (like Marx's laborer) the contradictions inherent in the production of America.[2] This is not to offer some new species of fetishism, to produce myself as some twenty-first century Norman Mailer, eager to maintain a too-easy distinction between self and other in a vain effort to pull from the margins of modern life some essential human "funkiness" that might save us all.[3] Instead, I echo the work of generations of feminists and black radicals who have insisted continuously that their visions of the American future are the most legitimately *American* visions now available to us. It is in this sense that this work is patently political. While it is full of equivocation and ambiguity, *Black Gay Man* is insistent in its defense of personal liberties, interracialism, internationalism, the security and dignity of our labor, and, yes, our America.

In this collection I attempt to bring together various elements of my political, cultural, and social identities—Perverse, Modern, American, Negro, Queer, Progressive—not as problems to be solved but as potentially fruitful ground for the articulation of American left identity. I do not wish to evoke anxiety or to demonstrate the difficulty of living with multiplicity, but rather to present its pleasure. I have made peace with the title of this work, *Black Gay Man*, not simply because of the guilty pleasure I take in registering the shock that it engenders in the largely academic, generally progressive circles in which I travel but also because of the way in which it returns me to the visceral, self-concerned, self-pleasuring bases for much of my activity as a left intellectual.

I am thinking now of one of my favorite sex partners, Rick, an ugly, poor, white trash southerner, with a scandalously thick Kentucky accent. What attracts me to Rick is precisely how ugly he is—bald head, chin pointing out too far, thin body, pale skin, shocking red hair bunched around a stubby, oddly shaped, and uncut cock. Rick reminds me of white boys from my youth, the ones so ugly and country that they seemed somehow to exist in another arena of whiteness, the ones from the edge of town who seemed always to own an old car in which occasionally they would shuttle me around like the prince of Egypt, the ones whom I sometimes saw hit each other in the mouth then cry and hug, all over some girl whom they were all too ugly to marry.

The image of Rick is infinitely disruptive. He knows that he is ugly, wears his knowledge like one of the fancy-dress uniforms left over from his days in the army. He loves sex, loves men's bodies, loves the sight of my face, loves to masturbate and moon over how beautiful I am, how fucking beautiful I am. When he comes, usually standing over me, jerking hard at his dick and making those strange moon faces, the liquid spills out almost like an accident. He drawls, "Goddamn, Goddamn," as the goo hits my skin. He then talks about Kentucky and poverty, about a mother with arthritis, about old boyfriends and the army, about no good relatives and abandoned children, about dreams for tomorrow, about me.

I am often asked to write about politics and culture, but I find that in most occasions the offer comes with the understanding that one will marshal the never fully stated but almost wholly appreciated modes of discretion, the deletion of pleasure, that work to keep most political writing decidedly dull and noncommital. The truth for me, however, is that there is no real disconnection in my mind among the political, the sexual, and the discursive, no real distinction between the particular and the universal. My commitments as a leftist intellectual come not in spite of the fact of my homosexuality or even my (perverse) desire for a certain class of ugly, southern white boy but in many ways because of these things. I understand my own cravings, preferences one might say, to be absolutely caught up in self-consciously produced and articulated political and intellectual identities: (interracialist, transnationalist, feminist, leftist). I believe that the image of Rick continues to be disruptive only insofar as one continues to support the false assumption that political identity is always the ultimate result of rational decision making and never a question of aesthetics, an act of self-pleasuring.

It has often been the case that individuals who have responded to previous versions of these essays remark the odd slippage in my writing between the academic and the pornographic, the rigorous and the soft. They have been surprised (pleasantly and otherwise) that I have attempted to refuse the easy distinctions between the political and the personal that continue to exist in so much of our work long after feminists presumably cleared the left intellectual environment of such odd notions. The disheartening thing for me is that although so many of us are inspired by the mundane, ever-present ache of desire (the will to be loved, to be seen, to be comforted, to be known), so few of us allow knowledge of that fact to seep into our writing. It is as if there is something so entirely decadent, so altogether provincial in our thirst for justice, for beauty, for fun that we attempt to cover our sinful flesh with an armor of rigor and sophistication.

I offer this image of Rick because I believe that in our struggle to produce an American progressivism we are lost if we discount the ways in which desire operates in the production of putatively rational decisions about government and politics. We risk the charge of hypocrisy if we offer only more and more sophisticated expressions of the anthropological gaze. We will clearly fail if we give into the fear that our dreams, our obsessions, our grubby secrets can never be vehicles for the articulation of the universal. This is not to say that I am naive enough to nominate sexual interaction between a black man and a white man as necessarily "queer," antinormative, transcendent, progressive. Still, I shudder at the thought of offering yet another rescripting of black identity that turns on the celebration of a never quite attainable, wholly sanitized, black normativity. I believe, in fact, that we will all have done a sorry job as intellectuals, as scholars, as teachers, as political activists, as members of the American public if we simply warm over versions of racial, sexual, and class difference that we ourselves find unpalatable.

In Washington we are obsessed with politics and sex, particularly the sex of powerful, coercive politicians. Yet a sort of dull, heavy silence falls most often around the politics—and the pleasure—of what we are doing, the humdrum perversities of our existence, the way we fuck. Our sexual politics tend most often to be trivialized into pornography or returned to darkness by an obscuring set of theoretical practices that demonstrate an incredible squeamishness about both sex and politics. As I come to understand that there is no easy distinction among my sex, my writing, and my politics, I find it easier to trust my intuition, to believe that when Rick, poor white, ugly, southern, hot Rick fucks me, something powerful happens. When we are together, we imagine, if only for a moment, a world transformed, a world so incredibly sexy and hot that the stupid, banal, and costly structures of racism, homophobia, poverty, and disease that work to keep us apart become nothing more than dully painful memories from the past.

In the nine essays that compose *Black Gay Man* I expend considerable energy attempting to articulate and dismantle these same structures. Specifically, I work in each essay to demonstrate the essentially permeable and thus impure nature of all American identities. Moreover, even as I demonstrate repeatedly the excessive lengths to which many have gone to reproduce the boundaries of various articulations of the self, I continue to emphasize my belief that the great joy of living in the modern world is the recognition that all processes of naming, all names (black, gay, man) are ultimately monuments to the impossibility of ever fully distinguishing self from other. In the countless articulations of race, gender, and sexuality that we have produced in American society, one always finds, rather easily I might add, counterarticulations of the same. We always find the universal.

I begin with "Speaking through Anti-Semitism," an examination of the ideological structures that motivate much of the inflammatory rhetoric that has emanated from the Nation of Islam. I argue that the fiercely anti-Semitic tone of many of the Nation's ministers speaks not to some free-floating "black anti-Semitism" in American society but instead to a real anxiety inside and outside the Nation that there are no real black boundaries, that it is altogether impossible to distinguish us from them. We all, it seems, are mixed. This anxiety is transferred onto the Jew, the interloper, not because he is so clearly different from the black but indeed because he is not different enough. His questionable genealogy, his history of oppression, his often intense religiosity are so very much like our own. It seems, in fact, that it is not until the moment of crisis, of attack, that one might find real distinctions. Indeed, the recurring crises between certain elements with black nationalist communities and certain elements within Jewish communities are necessary precisely because they *produce* distinction.

I continue in a somewhat similar vein with "Cosmopolitan Afrocentric Mulatto Intellectual." Reading two recent works that deal with the question of Black American intellectualism from the perspective of cosmopolitanism and Afrocentrism, respectively, I argue that, again, one finds in both traditions an abiding interest in the question of racial mixing. Rather in relation to the genealogies of key thinkers or as a problem in the production of Black American intellectual history, the mulatto and her place in the black family has captured the attention of many American intellectuals for centuries. Along with the mulatto, the Black American community has absorbed varieties of "blackness" into its distinctly American political and cultural structures. Thus, I tend to be not so quick to glibly dismiss Afrocentrism as an essentially

parochial tradition. Nor am I quite as eager as some others to celebrate the transcendent, "nonracial" nature of cosmopolitanism.
Instead, I argue that the power of the two texts that I examine is
that they demonstrate not only that Afrocentrism and cosmopolitanism are intimately related but that one cannot achieve
the universalist goals of the cosmopolitan without trafficking
with the particularist notions of the Afrocentrist.

"At Home in America" is a work in which I dwell on the radical consciousness of sixties and seventies black nationalists, particularly George Jackson and Malcolm X. In the process I refuse
their contention that the Black American is essentially an African
captive in this country and instead dwell upon the fact that indeed we are the most American of Americans, so much so that the
name Black American seems to me shockingly redundant. I go on
to argue that the intellectual structures that allow the notion of a
colonized "African" American community are heavily dependent
upon the erasure of much of actual American history. My abiding
interest in black nationalism stems, in fact, from the reality that
it is within this intellectual tradition that one sees the question of
the essential impurity, the perversity if you will, of the Black
American community to be taken up most consistently and in
many ways most seriously. Even as many black nationalists bemoan the Black American community as too light, too liberal, too
mute, and too mixed, they offer testament to the fact that the
Black American community not only is quintessentially modern
but has long wrestled with many of the questions of identity that
today plague many intellectuals in this country and elsewhere.

In the second section of essays, I demonstrate the manner in
which much of contemporary gay cultural and political life turns
upon the reproduction of the very assumptions of sexual and

racial difference that one finds in the rest of American society. In doing so, I suggest tentatively that gay sexual practice, even and especially when it is most caught up in the racialist nonsense that so overburdens our culture, offers the possibility of breaking through these same assumptions. In "Dinge" I examine the question of interracial sex in the gay community and the reproduction of White Hero, Black Beast mythology. With special attention to the work of James Baldwin, I suggest that the reproduction of racial mythologies, even and especially in our sex, has the potential to force recognition of the tedium of the American commonsense of race, sex, and sexuality. The ugly underside of this reality is the fact that those subjects presumably pressing against the norms of American communal life, those who keep mixed company, become symbols of the reality of the porous, penetrable nature of America and Americans and are thus often seized upon as titillating fetish objects rather than modern subjects creatively wrestling with the contradictions of their existence.

In "Tearing the Goat's Flesh," perhaps the most purely "literary" work within the collection, I work to offer a fresh reading of Eldridge Cleaver's *Soul on Ice*, Piri Thomas's *Down These Mean Streets*, and James Baldwin's *Giovanni's Room*. Still, I am more concerned to play out the theme of racial anxiety that I develop in earlier chapters. Specifically, I suggest that the homosexual, like the Jew, becomes in late-twentieth-century Black American writing a vehicle by which to express the omnipresence of the specter of black boundarylessness. At the same time, the process of his debasement, his abjection, produces for audiences tired of the commonsense of American racialism a glimpse at the possibilities just beyond our grasp, the world yet to be seen.

This world will not, I am afraid, be brought about by wands, wishes, or brisk clicks of the heels. It seems, in fact, that often those most capable of imagining a new mode of American "race relations" are those who give themselves over most fully to the racial fetishism that is so much a part of our culture. In "The Shock of Gary Fisher" I suggest not only that violence to black gay men, real and imagined, is an ugly cultural by-product in the production of American society but also that those black and white men involved in racialized sexual play run the risk of demonstrating the futility of all racial role playing. They demonstrate in their sometimes desperate attempts to reinscribe the racial commonsense what a tenuous grasp we all have on our (racial) identities. The black gay man is then an object of attack not because he represents that which is horrid but because he represents instead that which is appealing. He represents one location at which the possibility of choosing one's identity (even within the most oppressive conditions) becomes palpable.

In the final section of essays I suggest again that identity is not simply a conundrum to be solved but a location at which one might embrace the complexity of modern life. In "Living as a Lesbian" I celebrate the ability to play with identity first suggested to me in the work of many black lesbian writers. I play with the language of lesbianism and suggest that it is one useful vehicle, one of many, in our search for the universal. I argue that we ought think of lesbianism not as a reserve to be protected but as a potential, a state of joy, that each of us might achieve, if only for the briefest of moments.

This notion that the universal is not a fixed state of being but instead a passing phenomenon, a fleeting—if palpable—desire is more fully developed in "It's Raining Men." In this work I treat the Million Man March as both an example of race and sex anxiety and a marvelous spectacle of modern life. Again I suggest that the presence of black gay men in the Million Man March and elsewhere in American life is not an abomination (whether viewed from the perspective of religion-tinged conservatism or science-tinged progressivism) but, indeed, a promise. I argue further that, although the moments of transcendence that took place at the event were flawed and ephemeral, they were nonetheless infinitely valuable markers of the thirst within American culture for a just and peaceful society.

That the transcendent is not fixed but always fleeting, even peculiar, was a fact that I began to understand most fully after the death of my friend and comrade Essex Hemphill. I use the word "comrade" the way it was used by nationalists and revolutionists of the 1960s and 1970s to mean that I felt when with him that I was in the presence of a person bending the contradiction of his life into both beautiful art and revolutionary critique. I write in "A Child's Life" that at the moment I heard of Essex's death I immediately understood that my childhood had ended. His passing and that of my friends Marlon Riggs, Craig Harris, Assotto Saint, and Donald Woods, among many others, took away from me some of the most vivid examples of persons living their lives with something like freedom that I have ever seen. Their dying also alerted me to the seriousness of their endeavors. Each of them approached, encroached upon, occupied, and redeveloped space that was never meant for their use. They went to the center and squatted. This fact, more than anything else, contributed to the death by degrees that each of them suffered. These men were for me shining examples of visionary American intellectualism. Their deaths are ghastly monuments to the grotesque American tendency toward waste. In remembering them I am reminded always to be mindful not only of my time and talents but also of the incredible dangers that so many of us must daily confront simply to effect our survival.

Black Gay Man might be properly understood, then, as a settling of debts. It is at once an effort to refuse the tendency to look upon the foundations of my intellectual and social identity with skepticism and an effort to avoid getting caught in the trap of trivializing those foundations by refusing to build upon them. *Black Gay Man* is both a celebration of black gay male identity and a critique of the structures that allow for the production of that identity. To fully inhabit both positions, this unsettled space, is the most fitting monument that I can offer to the many individuals who have aided in my development as an intellectual and a citizen.

BLACK

Speaking through Anti-Semitism

All ideology represents in its necessarily imaginary distortion not the existing relations of production (and the other relations that derive from them), but above all the (imaginary) relationship of individuals to the relations of production. . . . What is represented in ideology is therefore not the system of the real relations which govern the existence of individuals, but the imaginary relation of those individuals to the real relations in which they live.

—LOUIS ALTHUSSER, "Ideology and Ideological
State Apparatuses"

You're not the true Jew. You are a Johnny-come-lately-Jew, who just crawled out of the caves and hills of Europe just a little over 4,000 years ago. You're not from the original people. You are a European strain of people who crawled around on your all fours in the caves and hills of Europe, eating Juniper roots and eating each other.

—KHALID ABDUL MUHAMMAD, speech at Kean College,
New Jersey, 11/29/93

It is amazing to consider how little we actually learned from the incredible controversy that gripped the nation following the shocking remarks of Khalid Muhammad, minister of the Nation of Islam, on the campus of Kean College in November 1993. It was not, of course, that no one paid attention, or that there was any reticence on the part of the variety of national elites to weigh in on the issue. On the contrary, op-ed pieces from the pens of literally dozens of prominent and not so prominent intellectuals appeared overnight on the pages of the country's newspapers and journals, while the U.S. Congress seemed to jump at the chance to censure both Muhammad and his spiritual leader, Minister Louis Farrakhan. What was surprising was not only what limited progress we made in our understanding of the sometimes difficult, often harmonious relationships between individual blacks and Jews but, more important, how underdeveloped our conceptual and theoretical apparatuses remained in relation to that rather ill-defined entity that captured, for a moment, the national imagination, "black anti-Semitism."

The phrase itself begs to be unpacked of all its manifold and often contradictory meanings. Is black anti-Semitism distinct from the plain old anti-Semitism practiced and preached by whites? Is it, in fact, Black American anti-Semitism, or are we to believe that the particular tensions that beset Black American/Jewish American relations in this country are replicated in communities of blacks and Jews throughout the world? Is it a contemporary phenomenon or an ancient aspect of black culture and consciousness? I cannot say that I have yet heard or read more than a cursory discussion of these issues. Instead, we have been treated repeatedly to what already seems a set of hackneyed and deeply functionalist readings of black/Jewish relations, readings that always seem to fall short of explaining the intensity with which the idea of black anti-Semitism has gripped our imaginations.

Blacks and Jews disagree, we are told, on Israel, Palestine, South Africa, affirmative action, school curricula, Jesse Jackson, and, of course, the Nation of Islam itself. More spiritually or philosophically minded commentators tend to focus on the presumably intense Christian religiosity of the black community, while those who favor structuralist approaches generally prefer rather mushy explanations of Jewish/black client relationships. The difficulty here is not so much that these observations are not based in reality. Indeed, the long and noble history of black and Jewish cooperation in the struggle for expanded civil rights and civil liberties aside, contentious exchanges between black and Jewish elites have been a regular part of the American landscape for at least the past thirty years. The anti-Israel statements made by some members of the Student Non-Violent Coordinating Committee in 1967 were reported widely in the press and criticized by a number of Jewish leaders. The struggle, in 1968, between the New York City teacher's union and black advocates of community school control clearly demonstrated deep cleavages in the old black/Jewish civil rights partnership. Andrew Young's meetings with members of the Palestine Liberation Organization, Jesse Jackson's "hymie-town" remark and, later, his association with Louis Farrakhan, the Leonard Jeffries debacle, and the Muhammad speech itself all point to general structural, cultural, and ideological differences between the black and the Jewish communities that become wildly apparent at moments of both national and local crisis. Still, it is worth making the point again that both the black and Jewish communities are veritable studies in complexity, ambiguity, and contradiction. One would be hard pressed to find consensus in either group around the myriad issues that beset them. In fact, it is a relatively easy task to find rather broad areas of overlap in the political and social concerns of blacks and Jews, particularly black and Jewish elites.

What continues to remain unexamined, however, is just why we are so shocked. Many people have asked why the anti-Semitism that emanates from within certain quarters of the black nationalist community has resulted in so much soul searching and hand wringing, while similarly vitriolic and hateful statements about Italians, gays and lesbians, and Arabs have remained largely unremarked. And perhaps more to the point is the related question of what is it about the figure of the Jew that so suits him as the bête noire of a certain black nationalist project when the relationship of Black Americans to both white Protestants and Catholics arguably has been and continues to be much more oppressive and demeaning. I have pointed already to the difficulty of trying to answer these questions through consideration of familiar black/Jewish political flash points. I also reject out of hand Andrew Hacker's contention that anti-Semitism allows blacks to align themselves more closely with white Protestants.[1] Indeed, Khalid Muhammad's words in relation to white South Africans— "We kill the women, we kill the children, we kill the babies. We kill the blind, we kill the crippled. . . . We kill the faggot, we kill the lesbian, we kill them all"—hardly seem designed to curry favor with white middle America. Thus, the idea that anti-Semitism among whites is somehow inversely proportionate to antiblack racism frankly seems nonsensical.

I suggest that we begin the process of understanding the contentiousness within black/Jewish relations—that is to say, unpacking what we mean, by "black anti-Semitism"—by pulling back for a moment, by refusing to accept the idea of anti-Semitism, or any form of racism for that matter, as a free-floating mode of signification by which various peoples express their anxiety and small-mindedness. The task that I have set out for myself is to understand anti-Semitism as an ideological structure, as one of the fictions by which many people, including Black American people, express our alienation within modern society. For this reason I began this essay by quoting a well-worn passage from Louis Althusser's "Ideology and Ideological State Apparatuses," a work in which Althusser forces us to an understanding of the fact that we create ideology, or alienated, imaginary representations of our social condition, precisely because the social condition is itself alienating. Furthermore, Althusser argues that it is ideology, through the complex process of interpellation, or hailing, that produces us as modern subjects.

I do recognize the danger of overdetermination in Althusser's work. I understand that the process of subjectification is quite a bit more complex and ambiguous than a simple procedure by which individuals are suited to social classes, or interpellated, through the ideological structures erected by state apparatuses and their adjuncts: the family, the church, social organizations, what have you. Still, I believe that Althusser's focus on alienation is particularly instructive for those of us interested in understanding modern black subjectivity. Indeed, as I argue later, the work of anti-Semitism, particularly as it has been expressed by some representatives of the Nation of Islam, is to express black alienation within the dominant narratives of modernity, narratives in which Jews and Jewishness figure centrally, if only as "threats, interlopers, or 'third subjects'" within the dominant structures of modern life, particularly the nation state.

It is my contention that when Khalid Muhammad, Leonard Jeffries, and Louis Farrakhan speak through anti-Semitism, they express not so much an antipathy for individual Jews as an antipathy for the structures of reason and civility by which anti-Semitic speech has been deemed destructive, dangerous, and, most important, irrational. Further, I suggest that the attraction for the black audience that finds itself enraptured by these men's diatribes is the thrill at seeing articulated within the public purview one's half-formed notions of existing not simply as an outsider within Western norms of civility and rationalism but as the very contradiction of those norms. What the Nation of Islam has done most successfully is to reshape the anxiety that the black subject exists only on the periphery of Western modernity into a general antipathy for the very structures of modernity, including the notions of civility and rationality that mitigate against anti-Semitic discourse and practice. What I take to be the tragedy of this mode of thought is not simply the ugly manner in which Jews have been used to express very real black alienation and scepticism in relation to the entire project of modernity—rationalism, civility, universalism—but also the fact that the focus upon the Jewish subject, especially in the manner practiced by Muhammad and Farrakhan, simply reiterates the tendency within the modern West to insist upon the bifurcation of the in and the out, the self and the other. The Jew remains the focus within the practice of what I am calling black countermodernity not so much because of the various "real-world" differences between many blacks and Jews but, on the contrary, because blacks and Jews are not different enough. The Jew is the interloper who disallows the easy delineation of the nation, the race, the people. As a consequence he must be cast out if "we" are to take form. "You're not the true Jew. You are a Johnny-come-lately-Jew, who just crawled out of the caves and hills of Europe just a little over 4,000 years ago."

Black Alienation

I think that at this point it is important for me to offer a caveat. I want to provide at least a partial answer to the critique that has been registered by almost every serious respondent to this essay during the several years since its first publication. In the pages that follow I make what I take to be a logical and principled argument about the way in which anti-Semitic rhetoric might properly be taken as an accurate measure of the level of alienation among some elements within the Black American community, particularly those most attracted to black nationalist movements and organizations. I must admit that this approach was designed first and foremost as a critique of those critics who attempted either to distinguish extreme elements in the Black American community (read poor and nationalist) from moderate ones (middle class and integrationist) or, conversely, to rehearse ad infinitum simpleminded versions of a rich-Jew-versus-impoverished-Negro narrative. What I saw and responded to were various versions of "voodoo criticism" in which not only all manner of pseudoscientific nonsense was offered up as fact ("Polls show that 'Black' Americans are twice as likely as their 'white' counterparts to make statements that might be taken as anti-Semitic.") but also in which the Black American was almost never understood as a subject of modern culture. In the absence of serious political and cultural critique, we were being offered images of a Black American community that was not so infinitely diverse that it is often nearly impossible to distinguish Black from white, Negro from Jew, but that was instead a flat, antiquated community stuck in provincialism, ecstatic religiosity, and intense xenophobia. In short, the black was always understood as the primitive.

I think that the arguments that follow continue to stand on their own merits, and I make no apologies for them here. I will say, however, that, while I maintain that black anti-Semitic rhetoric and the alienation that it demonstrates ought to be taken as markers of the black's complex relationship to modernity, this does not mean that I wish to celebrate so-called Black anti-Semitism. On the contrary, my thrust in this essay and those that follow is precisely to suggest that the Black American is not alien in this nation. Much of the work of *Black Gay Man*, in fact, is to suggest the very term "Black American" is a study in the redundant and the tautological; the Black American as the *American* American. The anti-Semitism of groups like the Nation of Islam stems directly from a desire to deny this fact, to contradict the reality of the Black American's modernity, her universality. The bombastic statements of Khalid Muhammad or Minister Farrakhan all turn on the notion that we are essentially an innocent people, out of place in this country. Consequently, our purity, our status as supposed Africans, might be precisely measured by the amount we are able to shock so-called polite American society.

One is not forced to look far in order to find rather startling critiques by black intellectuals of the narratives—and narrators—that have helped define modernity. Indeed, no less a critic than Henry Louis Gates has devoted much of his professional life to coming to terms with the fact that from its inception in the late eighteenth century the black literary project has been self-consciously concerned not only with demonstrating through literature and literacy the necessity—and the inevitability—of recognizing black subjectivity and individuality, but also with breaking the black/white binarism in which the bestiality of the black acts as proof of the white's humanity. Gates writes:

*Unlike almost every other literary tradition, the Afro-American literary tra-
dition was generated as a response to eighteenth—and nineteenth—century
allegations that persons of African descent did not, and could not, create literature. Philosophers and literary critics, such as Hume, Kant, Jefferson,
and Hegel, seemed to decide that the absence or presence of a written literature was the signal measure of the potential, innate humanity of a race.
The African living in Europe or in the New World seems to have felt compelled to create a literature both to demonstrate implicitly that blacks did
indeed possess the intellectual ability to create a written art and to indict
the several social and economic institutions that delimited the humanity of
all black people in Western cultures.*[2]

Gates's point is well taken. For it points both to the continual
need for black intellectuals to produce work that speaks to the
reality that indeed we are human beings and to the rather contradictory and troubling fact that we have been forced to ac-
complish this task, this articulation of our humanity, within
modes of discourse that are deeply flawed precisely because
they are constructed upon a denial of this humanity. The struggle for the black intellectual has been to exist at once inside and
outside the norms of rationality constructed by the major authors of modern thought. Gates himself has attached the label
"signifyin'" to this process. At the same time, he has identified
a second strain within black thought that would deny the
black's implication within modernity altogether, stressing instead a black ontology that both predates and supercedes white
Western culture. For Gates, this line of thinking is best represented by the Black Arts Movement and Negritude, both of
which were concerned with delineating the parameters of an
ancient black consciousness that is literally carried about
within the bodies of the individual members of the African

diaspora. More recently, certain strains of Afrocentrism have proceeded in much the same manner. In this way, blackness becomes a powerful living entity, one that expresses itself, for those capable of reading and understanding it, in a remarkably predictable and static manner. The quality of black literature and art can be judged then by how closely it conforms to black experience, an experience that stands in contradistinction to the norms of the white West.

This is the intellectual context out of which the Black Muslim movement and, later, the Nation of Islam developed in the Detroit of the 1930s, a time described by C. Eric Lincoln, perhaps still the most thoughtful student of the Black Muslims, as one of "hunger, confusion, disillusionment, despair, and discontent."[3] More to the point, Black Americans who, along with the rest of the world, were about to witness a shockingly deep economic crisis, the depression, and even deeper political and social crises, World War II and the Holocaust, had themselves just begun to turn the tide against both economic violence and systematic attacks by white terrorists, particularly lynching, a practice that largely defined American race relations from the turn of the century forward. To add insult to injury, the black community, which had distinguished itself in the struggle against German aggression during World War I, found that, as black soldiers returned after their loyal service in the cause of justice and democracy, their new-found sense of self and sense of investment in the national project were resented and resisted by their white compatriots. Lynchings continued apace, with reports of several returning soldiers being tortured and killed while still in uniform. Every black person could expect, per usual, to be segregated, disenfranchised, economically exploited, and then blamed for the supposed failures of his community. What is surprising, then, is not so much that one might have found at this time antidemocratic elements within the black community but, on the contrary, that Black Americans continued to cling so tenaciously to the democratic project, even as the white American disciples of democracy attacked and consistently exploited our various communities, often going so far as to deny our very humanity.

It follows that when the mysterious and racially ambiguous W. D. Fard began meeting with small groups of the most oppressed members of the black community in the ghettos of Detroit, telling them that they belonged to a tradition that was older, more noble, more innocent and ultimately more democratic than the system of Western rationalism and universality that they recognized as so clearly flawed, he found an audience that was altogether ready to receive and accept his message. Fard's mixture of Christian and Moslem theology, his insistence that the Black American community was not isolated but deeply connected to the rest of the "Asiatic" world, a point to which we return later, and his scathing attacks on white hypocrisy earned for him a place of honor among many of Detroit's black citizens. It is important to remember in this context that Fard's mission—which would later develop, largely through the efforts of Elijah Muhammad, into the Nation of Islam—was itself part of a larger black spiritual, religious, and social movement that included Marcus Garvey's Universal Negro Improvement Association, The Moorish Science Temples, led by the Noble Drew Ali, the United African Nationalist Movement, and even Rastafarianism, which was soon to become a major force in much of the English-speaking Carribean, especially Jamaica. All of these movements stressed the need for blacks to reintegrate themselves into a tradition of what one might think of as black nobility, while severing their enervating and demeaning connections to whites. The impressive public spectacles of the Garvey movement, for example, were designed to make palpable the extraordinary nature of the so-called colored community in the face of constant and systematic demoralization.

Modernity and Ambivalence

It is the will to separate, to define oneself in contradistinction to whiteness that stands, I believe, at the center of the anti-Semitism that has emanated out of the Nation of Islam. It is, moreover, this very desire for clear definition that marks the movement as precisely a modern phenomenon, caught up, interestingly enough, in the same ideological structures of modernity against which it purports to struggle. I have been influenced in this regard by the work of Zygmunt Bauman, particularly his *Modernity and Ambivalence*.[4] Therein Bauman suggests that modernity is defined by the unrelenting desire, on the part of its architects, to order the world, to clearly delineate the good from the bad, the self from the other. In the process, however, one constantly encounters ambivalence; rather, the process of definition constantly engenders ambivalence, thus trapping us within an endless cycle of definition and redefinition. In this schema, the phenomena that the modern subject must struggle against, must seek to erase, are not those things that can be defined clearly as bad, or evil, but instead that which cannot be defined at all, those phenomena that exist outside the purview of rationalism altogether, thereby calling into question the validity of modern modes of inquiry and understanding. Bauman writes:

The typically modern practice, the substance of modern politics, of modern intellect, of modern life, is the effort to exterminate ambivalence: an effort to define precisely—and to suppress or eliminate everything that could not or would not be precisely defined. Modern practice is not aimed at the conquest of foreign lands, but at the filling of the blank spots in the compleat mappa mundi. *It is modern practice, not nature, that truly suffers no void. (Bauman, 7–8)*

In this regard, Bauman (who is also the author of *Modernity and the Holocaust*) suggests that Jews and gypsies represent a threat to the structures of modernity, particularly the nation state, because they somehow seem to escape the yoke of definition. As Bauman argues, the Jew is conceptualized as the stranger, the "as-yet-decided," the "premonition of that 'third element' which should not be." The logic of anti-Semitism proceeds from the fear not simply that Jews represent a nation within a nation, as it were, but that it is impossible to pinpoint exactly *what* they represent. Into this void the anti-Semite deposits a conception of the Jew as devil or saint precisely to mitigate against Jewish inconclusivity.

Before I leave this subject, I would like to gesture for a moment to Sander Gilman's rather remarkable work in relation to the process by which both Jews and blacks are pathologized within western thought. The striking thing is that the distinction between the black and the Jew is altogether fuzzy and inconclusive within racist ideology. Gilman points to many instances in which the Jew is conceptualized as some highly diluted or reified manifestation of the black. Indeed, the belief that Jews are not white stands at the center of much of anti-Semitic thought and continues as a signal element within Jew bashing, even in this country, even today. The sad aspect of all this is that so many of us—blacks, Jews, and gentiles of all races—spend such inordinate amounts of energy debating the fiction of race. Indeed, this conflation of blackness and Jewishness is precisely the site of ambiguity that has been reacted against so vigorously by members of the Nation of Islam. I remind you here of the fact that early in the Nation's history its members were invited to imagine themselves as "Asiatic" while at the same time being pushed to sever their ties to other races of people, particularly whites. The effect has been to produce a sort of cultural schizophrenia in which, on the one hand, an identity that is imagined as larger than blackness is celebrated, while, on the other, very few others are allowed to share this identity. Thus, we find the odd response to the Nation's critics that Black Americans cannot be anti-Semitic because we are ourselves Semites. This particularly complex and rich ideological structure is what I believe Minister Farrakhan references when he argues that the purpose of the Nation's wildly controversial book, *The Secret Relationship Between Blacks and Jews*, published in 1991 by the Nation itself, was to "rearrange a relationship that has been detrimental to us." This rearrangement, I argue, has been calculated to demolish the ambiguity that the Jew represents in relation to the black community, to reorder somehow the reality that Jews and blacks always seem to inhabit an intimate space in which they are at once the best of friends and the worst of enemies.

The Secret Relationship

That *The Secret Relationship* is limited as a piece of scholarship is an irrefutable claim. There is almost no effort on the part of the authors to move their arguments forward, paying attention along the way to the subtleties of the topics with which they are engaged. In this work there is an absence of narrative progression. We are assured at the beginning of the text that Jews were disproportionately represented within the slave trade and reassured of the same at the end.

Deep within the recesses of the Jewish historical record is the irrefutable evidence that the most prominent of the Jewish pilgrim fathers used kidnaped Black Africans disproportionately more than any other ethnic or religious group in New World history and participated in every aspect of the international slave trade.[5]

The Secret Relationship is really a compendium of evidence documenting Jewish involvement in the pernicious practice with little differentiation between various groups or individuals. Jewish slave traders in Curacao look exactly like Jewish financiers in Brazil, who for their part replicate Jewish plantation owners in the Old South, Martinique, and so forth. What is perhaps even more interesting about this text, however, is what at first seems the strange historiographic practice of its anonymous authors. With more than 1,200 notes that reference an impressive pool of scholars, whom we are assured are almost exclusively Jewish, the work attempts, interestingly enough, to shield itself from the charge of anti-Semitism even in the midst of the most horrid accusations against Jewish people. At the same time, there is almost no notice taken of the rather impressive body of work that has been produced by black scholars that speaks not only to the horrors of slavery and the slave trade but also and importantly to black resistance in all its myriad forms. Indeed, this seems beside the point. The narrative that the Nation has constructed is one in which enslaved Africans never took action within the historical dramas in which they were enmeshed. On the contrary, all activity is reserved for Jews. Jews are guilty moderns. Blacks are innocent primitives. In fact, the vitriolic and bombastic rhetoric of the text would have one believe that only with its publication have black people struck the first blow for their freedom.

Thus, what we gain through consideration of *The Secret Relationship*'s structure is a better understanding of the ideological work that the text is designed to do. Following Althusser, I have argued that ideology works to produce subjects through a process of interpellation, or hailing. He writes:

ideology "acts" or "functions" in such a way that it "recruits" subjects among the individuals (it recruits them all) by that very precise operation which I have called interpellation *or hailing, and which can be imagined along the lines of the most commonplace everyday police (or other) hailing: "Hey, you there!"* [6]

The obvious response to this claim would be that the authors of *The Secret Relationship* are attempting to hail the Jewish subject. "Hey, you, you are the one who stole us from Africa, stripped us of our dignity and kept your foot solidly on our necks." What is less obvious is the manner in which the black subject is being hailed. If you accept the argument that I have just made about the relative lack of agency assigned to the black victims of slavery by the authors of *The Secret Relationship,* then what becomes apparent is that the individuals whom the Nation is recruiting are alienated not simply from the norms of Western modernity but from the reality of their own history, as well. Thus, the real indictment of the Jewish stranger, the interloper, is that he keeps the innocent black nation from finding itself.

Indeed, the Jew is depicted throughout the text as the very antithesis of the nationalist. His identity always supercedes nationalism, so much so, in fact, that he always can be expected to act on this prior identity, even if it involves treachery to the nation to which he nominally belongs.

The Gentiles were, for the most part, nationalists, owing their allegiance to the nation in whose territory they resided. They respected the edicts of their government particularly with regard to international relations. The Jews, on the other hand, considered themselves as Jews first, particularly in international commerce. They remained internationalists without the patriotic fervor of their Gentile countrymen. (The Secret Relationship, *25)*

Presumably, the Civil War divided the country, "pitting brother against brother," in a bitter ideological battle. Not so among the country's Jews, who carried on lively interaction, social and commercial. Northern Jewish congregations "responded generously" to the call for help from their brethren in the Confederacy. (The Secret Relationship, *156)*

These claims replicate, of course, long standing stereotypes about Jews and Jewishness. Yet I suggest again that the focus is not so much on individual Jews or on real-world black/Jewish relations. Again, these seem beside the point. The anxiety that is being expressed here is an anxiety engendered by the confusion surrounding the reasons that the nation promised by W. D. Fard, Elijah Muhammad, Marcus Garvey, and Malcolm X, has been so long coming and seems so unlikely to ever arrive.

If we can disengage for a moment from the particular sting we feel when we hear that it is the Jew who keeps the black oppressed, what we find is very real angst and melancholy, in a word alienation, in relation to the black experience of modernity. There is a sense of bewilderment, of hurt, that one hears in the voices of black people, particularly young black people, when we ask ourselves, If the Jews could do it, then why can't we? Of course, this line of thinking emanates from the very tendency identified by Gates, among others, to deny the culture and history of Africans in the diaspora, to point to the black past and find only lack, or, in the case of the Nation and a variety of other black nationalist organizations, an image of black culture and consciousness so noble and transcendent, so innocent that it does little to actually address the needs and everyday concerns of contemporary Black Americans. In either case, the actual history of Africans in the diaspora seems to begin at this historical moment. Blacks become associated with the all too apparent breakdown of modernity and the variety of modern structures. Much of the discussion around the erosion of our cities, for example, turns precisely upon racist notions regarding those cities' largely black populations. As I have argued throughout this essay, the response to this reality by some black nationalist intellectuals has been to turn the standard narrative of modernity on its head, to suggest that the horror of modernity should be represented not by the black but by the Jew.

Holocaust

The Secret Relationship ends with a section entitled, "Jews of the Black Holocaust," a phrase that violently collapses the several focuses of the work in upon themselves. In a bizarre twist of logic, Jews cease to be the victims of holocaust and become instead its perpetrators. The section essentially replicates the structure of the rest of the work, offering short descriptions of individual Jews who purportedly were involved in slavery.

David Namias was a Barbados planter in 1680 'with a dozen Negroes and twenty acres of land.' His household in St. Michaells [sic] housed nine persons (Jews) and five further slaves.'

David De Isaac Cohen Nassy of Philadelphia held two 'personal slaves' (which is synonymous with 'sexual slave'). His Jewish ancestors built a whole colony in Surinam based on African slave labor.

Asher Moses Nathan of Baton Rouge, Louisiana was a businessman who loaned money to plantation owners for slave buying and was himself a slave dealer. He owned an eighty-year-old Black male whom Nathan attempted to sell when he fell ill in 1807. This practice, in another instance, netted his estate $72 when he sold a 70 year old Black woman named 'Lucretia.' (The Secret Relationship, *287)*

This laundry list of Jewish slavers not only completes *The Secret Relationship;* it also offers us an extremely useful foothold in our effort to make sense of the text. The reader is expected to become bewildered and enraged at the depth of Jewish involvement in the slave trade. The list proceeds relentlessly, with Jew after Jew indicted for the exploitation, rape, and murder of African captives. In the process it displaces the Jewish experience of Holocaust as the moment that defines the ugly underside of modernity and suggests, nay, insists that the slave experience proves that modernity has been flawed from its very inception. This pairing of slavery and holocaust suggests that somehow the shocking and grotesque events of the Second World War were themselves inevitable, given Jewish culpability in the earlier and more profound tragedy of slavery. I do not feel it necessary to repeat at this juncture Khalid Muhammad's musing about the greatness of Hitler or the treachery of Jews in Nazi Germany. I would, however, like to reiterate my point about the rather tired manner in which the text continues a false binarism in which the Jew is oppressor, the black victim. In this manner, *The Secret Relationship* almost perfectly replicates the long-since debunked claims of Stanley Elkins, who argues in his 1959 work, *Slavery: a Problem in American Institutional and Intellectual Life*, that the slave community did not struggle but instead reverted to a sort of childlike dependency within its completely controlled and oppressive environment.[7] Interestingly enough, he takes the concentration camp as the model by which to construct his analysis.

The obvious flaws within this line of thinking have been demonstrated by at least three generations of historians. Elkins is often taught, in fact, as an example of poorly conceived method and practice. Still, it seems to me that his thesis, as limited as it is, does point to a noble desire on the part of a minority of scholars to think through the implications of slavery and the Holocaust at the same time. The fact that so little real work has been done on this issue has left not only black and Jewish intellectuals but all of us concerned with understanding the nature of modernity in a sort of no-man's land in which there is a largely unspoken, if widespread, resentment that our tragedy is not recognized as *the* tragedy. This reality leads, I believe, not only to the strange pseudoscholarship represented within *The Secret Relationship*, but, more important, to the continuation of the false binarisms, the us-and-them mentality, that allowed these horrors to be visited upon our various peoples in the first place. Moreover, as Paul Gilroy has suggested in his critique of Zygmunt Bauman, scholars of modernity consistently have missed the opportunity to deepen their understanding of their subject precisely because they have been unable, because of racism, Eurocentrism, or what have you, to see the striking similarities between Jews and Africans in the New World. The themes of diaspora, exile, slavery, tradition, social memory, and redemption are central to both intellectual traditions. There is, in fact, so much overlap that it is difficult, upon consideration, to clearly delineate one from the other. The task before us, then, is to embrace this ambiguity, to come to terms with the process of constantly recreating who we are, not striking out against that which is unfamiliar, that which cannot be familiarized, but learning to accept the constant crossing of boundaries that is the hallmark of our condition.

Coda

In listening to myself, within this essay, I am struck by the fact that I have been concerned exclusively with what I have called "black anti-Semitism" and have not offered a word on that equally slippery and sinister entity, "Jewish racism." Part of the reason for this is that by training and inclination I am a scholar of Black American experience and subjectivity, and, although I believe my work speaks to many people, I have throughout this essay imagined my audience as primarily black, progressive, and anti-anti-Semitic. Further, I do take the notion of a specifically Jewish racism as a question and not a foregone conclusion, though if there is such a thing my suspicion is that the ideological structure that it represents is roughly analogous to the one that I have just described. I have followed this particular line of inquiry not simply because I believe that anti-Semitism from any quarter is morally reprehensible but also because I believe that it retards the further advancement of Black Americans. I want to be certain, however, that my work is not taken as further evidence of the false notion that Black Americans are a particularly anti-Semitic people. Indeed, this line of thought always has seemed to me to be a bit of rank racism, one that deserves to be driven out—along with the notion of our intense homophobia and misogyny—into the graveyard of antiblack ideas where presumably you will find all those tails that we used to grow after midnight and all those extra tendons that made us jump so highly, run so quickly, and bow so deeply.

Those of us who count ourselves as progressive scholars and intellectuals cannot afford to so belittle the reality of anti-Semitism that we cease to understand it as one of the primary technologies of terror and dominance within Western culture and instead imagine it as the simple and awkward ranting of less advanced sectors of the population. It is my fear that anti-Semitism will be allowed to grow within white communities precisely because it has now become so convenient to locate it among blacks. At the same time, it seems increasingly true that the nation's antiblack racism is piggybacked onto Jewish responses to what has been imagined as an onslaught of black anti-Jewish rhetoric. I am supported in these claims by an episode of the *Phil Donahue Show* that aired on March 20, 1995, and that was titled "Blacks and Jews against Each Other," in which a group of rather buffoonish blacks and Jews took turns attacking one another. The striking thing to me was that almost no one on the panel actually represented anything even approaching mainstream black or Jewish thought. Among the black guests were Shaharazad Ali, who came to national prominence by suggesting that black men should beat black women, and Tony Martin, whose book, *The Jewish Onslaught: Despatches from the Wellesley Battlefront* turns his career difficulties into an indictment of all Judaism.[8] The group was rounded out by a rabbi who balked at the idea of afterschool programs in which black and Jewish children might indiscriminately play basketball together and the "reasonable" panelists, one of whom insisted that Jews control the media, the other, a New York City Council member, who called for blacks to come to grips with our presumably intense Jewish envy. The point that I am attempting to make here is the same one that many others have made before me. The ongoing public strife between blacks and Jews is not designed to further the ends of either community. In fact, exactly the opposite is true. In every respect, these flareups help only to substantiate the half-formed racist notions that people carry about who we are. Indeed, instead of sponsoring solid debate and inquiry, the media have been concerned primarily with reifying tensions between blacks and Jews in such a manner that public dialogue becomes impossible. The work that stands before us, then, is precisely to work, to go beyond the practice of simply throwing a few good vibes in the direction of the opposing camp, and instead to insist upon a thorough reconceptualization of both the ways in which we communicate and the manner in which we constitute ourselves as individuals and communities. I hope that these brief comments have been a step forward in that direction.

II   Cosmopolitan Afrocentric Mulatto Intellectual

> Africa is still chained to Europe, and exploited by Europe, and
> Europe and America are chained together; and as long as this is
> so, it is hard to speak of Africa except as a cradle and a potential.
> —JAMES BALDWIN, *The Price of the Ticket*

The rather daunting challenge of reading Ross Posnock's *Color and Culture: Black Writers and the Making of the Modern Intellectual* in relation to Wilson Jeremiah Moses's *Afrotopia: The Roots of African American Popular History* is the necessity of coming to terms with both writers' insistence that categories generally understood as mutually exclusive—black and intellectual, Afrocentrism and cosmopolitanism—are so intimately intertwined as to make them indistinguishable. The payoff, however, is in the fact that in reading these works one is brought that much closer to a clear understanding not only that the black subject might be recognized as the universal subject but also that her universalism is itself always channeled through the reality of her particularity, the fact of blackness. Whether represented through the figure of a W. E. B. Du Bois forced by racism and provincialism to complete much of his formal study in Europe or a Samuel Delany bent on reshaping the lie of race into a constantly evolving process of self-creation, many Black American intellectuals have staked out remarkably powerful intellectual positions in which the most despised subjects of the state have dared suggest themselves the most capable citizens of the nation. Posnock and Moses demonstrate that black intellectuals have maintained in the face of the most horrid abuses a profound belief in the universal and the cosmopolitan while never quite giving up on the notion of black peculiarity.

Ross Posnock's refreshing critique of the idea that the black intellectual is a new and extraordinary phenomenon gains much of its force from his careful unpacking of American intellectual genealogies. He reminds us that the concept of the intellectual was transplanted from Europe into America largely via the efforts of twentieth-century black writers, particularly Du Bois, in a conscious effort to produce the self-consciously politicized intellectualism on display during the Dreyfus Affair. Similarly, Wilson Moses insists that we understand the intellectual tendencies and traditions loosely grouped under the rubric of Afrocentrism as part of a much longer process, one that has its roots deep in the cultural and social histories of both Europe and America. Specifically, he reiterates a previously made but I believe never fully appreciated observation that not only have many of the central figures of Afrocentrism been self-identified as European or Euro-American (Boas, Herskovits, Malinowski) but a significant portion might be properly understood to have been apologists for both racial segregation and slavery (Herder, Gobineau, Robert Park).

In making these claims, Posnock and Moses regularly return—directly and indirectly—to the question of the mulatto. Posnock expends considerable energies trying to make sense of the articulation of mulatto status by "black" intellectuals such as Du Bois, Jean Toomer, and, more recently, Samuel Delany and Adrian Kennedy, while Moses paints a picture of nineteenth- and twentieth-century black intellectualism that presents the broadly grinning face of white "benefactors" at almost every turn. The mulatto becomes then an actual impediment in the production of a black intellectual history. Douglass, Du Bois, James Weldon Johnson, Walter White, Alain Locke, Booker T. Washington, and a host of other black writers, educators, and political activists could have been—and often were— identified as mulatto at least until 1920, when the category was dropped from the American census. Thus, if we are to accept the notion of black intellectualism as it has been articulated by Posnock and Moses, it begs the question of whether there can be a black intellectualism, including Afrocentrism, that is not already a mulatto intellectualism.

One might even go so far as to ask whether the import of both men's work is their radical reconfiguration of Black American intellectual genealogies such that the 1920s become not so much a moment in which Black intellectuals come to recognize the essential Africanity of their culture but instead one in which black intellectuals in concert with white social scientists begin the very difficult cultural and social work of erasing the distinction between black and mulatto and rigidifying the distinction between the "purely" black and the wholly "white." This idea, one that is suggested forcefully in the work of both scholars, is compelling because it disallows the still widely held notion that black intellectual movements such as the Harlem Renaissance represent a return to a black and African originality that somehow had been lost by earlier generations of Black Americans. Specifically, it insists that the expression of black identity, even putatively Afrocentric expression, was always a cosmopolitan (that is to say, interracial, transnational) affair.

At the same time, I believe that one of the more startling implications of Posnock's and Moses's work is that cosmopolitanism, even as it is prescribed as an anecdote to feverishly parochial concepts of self, may have its roots deep in the production of the same provincialisms that it is expected to overcome. Can there be a cosmopolitanism in the absence of Afrocentrism? Can there be a cosmopolitan who is not mulatto? Is the sense of vertigo invoked by the appellation "cosmopolitan Afrocentric mulatto intellectual" a factor of our recognition of the improbability of the notion, or our shock at its over determination?

I began with this line of thinking almost from the first moment of reading Posnock's *Color and Culture*.[1] As I have stated already, I was particularly taken with his clever rescripting of twentieth-century intellectual history in which he suggests Du Bois as a primary conduit between the Dreyfusards of turn-of-the-century France and modern American writers. On the one hand, he insists upon the importance of a black, or rather a mulatto (the waffling on this point continues even today), in the reproduction of the notion of the intellectual as politically engaged cosmopolitan. On the other, he reminds us that there was never a pure moment of either American or European intellectualism in which pernicious distinctions of race and ethnicity did not exist. The Dreyfus Affair was fueled by the deeply rooted anti-Semitism of *fin de siècle* France and the cosmopolitan, universalist response of French intellectuals, particularly Zola. Posnock rightly celebrates their efforts to give voice to "humankind's sense of justice and humanity against the anti-Semitism of French nationalists" (2). He then goes on to remind us that the word "intellectual" comes into modern political and cultural discourse as a slur against the Dreyfusards, who were branded both "*intellectuels*" and "*déracinés*."

I believe that it would be a mistake for us to read this initial moment in the production of the modern intellectual as one in which the artists and professionals involved bounded above the fray of race and ethnicity. Though it is somewhat appealing to suggest that we collapse the notion of the intellectual and the deracinated, I continue to harbor a fair amount of skepticism about whether this actually gets at what was being expressed by either the Dreyfusards or their detractors. It seems perfectly plausible that the notion of deracination gained its force primarily from its currency in European and American culture as an aspersion properly reserved for Jews, a community understood as being without nation, language, or culture of its own, one that was feared because it was at once largely indistinguishable from the rest of the population and yet somehow different. Posnock properly quotes Habermas in his articulation of the anxiety that was invoked by the production of the idea of the modern intellectual: "Both sides fear from the intellectual the mixing of categories that would do to remain separate" (quoted in Posnock, 2). It is imperative, I believe, that we understand that this fear of mixing is in many ways indistinguishable from the fear of racial mixing that has preoccupied Western intellectuals, including Black American intellectuals, for at least the past three centuries. The fact that Habermas takes up this issue in a discussion of German phobias surrounding culture, nationality, and the role of the intellectual already seems to me to beg the question. One might argue, in fact, that perhaps the most profound legacy of German intellectualism is the intensity of its response to questions of pollution and impurity. To put the matter bluntly, the specter who hides just below the surface of much of the discourse of Western intellectualism (German, American, or otherwise) is indeed the mulatto.

This point was hardly lost on the twentieth-century "black" writers whom Posnock celebrates. In one of the most jarring moments in Posnock's text, he introduces a striking passage from one of Du Bois's journals, detailing his journey home aboard a passenger ship after two years in Europe.

In his notebook Du Bois differentiates himself as one of three mulattoes from "two full-blooded Negroes" who are also passengers. "We do not go together." Herbert Aptheker, when he edited the posthumously published Autobiography, *revised this passage to read: "There are five Negroes aboard. We do not go together." [David Levering] Lewis provides the original text to preserve Du Bois's distinction. For Lewis, that distinction indicates a "subtext of proud hybridization . . . so prevalent in Du Bois's sense of himself that the failure to notice it in the literature about him is as remarkable as the complex itself." . . . Lewis wonders if there is not a "deeper culpability," "a wilfully arrogant . . . standing apart as a different breed from the great majority of the people of the race he believed it his destiny to uplift?" (Posnock, 112)*

It seems unavoidable that students of American intellectual history will feel compelled to take up the gauntlet that David Levering Lewis has thrown down, particularly those who wrap themselves in the mantle of cosmopolitanism. There is indeed no manner in which one might neatly extricate Du Bois's intellectualism from his racialism. He clearly relishes his identity both as a cosmopolitan and as a mulatto. It is important to remember, though, that Du Bois, his peers, his followers, and their detractors did not simply import American racialism into a pristine European

cosmopolitanism. Instead, they found the notion of the culturally hybrid mulatto to be absolutely resonant with the notion of
the culturally hybrid intellectual. It is telling that the clash between the hybrid and the pure, the mixed and the "full-blooded,"
occurs on board a ship, that location that has become for many
American intellectuals the very emblem of the possibilities inherent within cosmopolitan intellectualism.[2]

It is here that I find myself somewhat confused by Posnock's
treatment of a number of the individuals whom he discusses
within the pages of *Color and Culture*. He works assiduously to
demonstrate the incredible lengths to which his representative
group of black writers has gone in order to move beyond the veil
of race, to place themselves and their ideas in a realm above the
reach of gross physiological and ethnic distinction. Yet the evidence that he marshals consistently demonstrates that these writers were less concerned with the question of racelessness than
many of their students seem to be today. The effect is that one is
left with the distinct feeling that Posnock is always arguing for a
rather straightforwardly positivistic understanding of "black" intellectual history, one in which a variety of writers used their various racial identifications as but launching points for their jour-
neys toward a raceless cosmopolitanism.

In discussing Ralph Ellison's admiration for Alain Locke, the
full force of Posnock's considerable argumentative abilities seems
to have been turned toward demonstrating that the clearly racialist arguments that Ellison and Locke put forward are important
precisely insofar as they announce their own obsolescence.

Locke's anti-purist pluralism helped Ellison and his friend Albert Murray
see that "all blacks are part white, and all whites part black." Locke came

to the fore in that 1920s moment of "turbulent transition," just "when we were far enough away from the traumas of Reconstruction" to broaden perspectives. As early as 1916 Locke had argued that when "modern man talks about race" he is really talking about ethnic groups, which Locke labeled "ethnic fictions" to expose the "fetish of biological purity" animating such terminology. In fact, ethnic groups are "the products of countless interminglings . . . the results of infinite crossings." By 1925, as editor of The New Negro, *Locke had sponsored a collective cultural practice that enacted his dismissal of purity. In the 1960s and 1970s Ellison watched with dismay the retreat to purism, to the ethnic province of "blood magic and blood thinking." (Posnock, 16–17)*

Posnock's description of Ellison's relation to Locke seems to me to be correct in almost all its particulars. Yet the logic that drives his argument continues to be difficult for me to grasp. Though Ellison may have decried the "blood thinking" of late-twentieth-century black nationalists, this does not mean that he himself was not concerned with the issue of blood. To say that all whites are part black and all blacks part white is nowhere near saying that there is simply no such thing as the black or the white. Indeed, the critique of the fetish of biological purity, the emphasis on intermingling and crossings, might be properly understood as Ellison's and Locke's attempts to reinvigorate a racialized (mulatto) cosmopolitanism in relation to the newly achieved nationalist provincialisms of twentieth-century Black America.

More directly, I suggest that Ellison's aesthetic and political concerns were precisely to understand his ethnicity, his identity as a Negro, not as thing which might be discounted, shrugged off like a soiled garment, but instead the very vehicle by which one might gain access to the universal. Much of the rhetorical power of his collection of essays and interviews, *Shadow and Act*, rests in his insistence that Negro identity is not limiting but instead presents a wide open door to the cosmopolitan and the ecumenical.

being a Negro American involves a willed *(who wills to be a Negro? I do!) affirmation of self as against all outside pressures—an identification with the group as extended through the individual self which rejects all possibilities of escape that do not involve a basic resuscitation of the original American ideals of social and political justice. And those white Negroes (and I do not mean Norman Mailer's dream creatures) are Negroes too—if they wish to be.*[3]

Ellison takes "Negro" identity to be a particularly precious aspect of American life. For him there is no question of Negro tradition and community, but these realities are only partly bounded by blood. Indeed, for Ellison, one's status as a Negro American is essentially a choice. "Who wills to be a Negro?" The query is itself an insistent articulation of the notion that Negroes are not those people trapped by biology within an historical drama that they can never affect. Instead, for Ellison, the articulation of Negro identity is first and foremost a reaffirmation of "the original American ideals of social political justice." Thus, the Negro is not born per se but *reborn* out of the detritus of American racialism. It is not so much a matter of deracination as *re*racination, the production of the Negro as a marker of the universal and the cosmopolitan such that even the "whitest" individual (the mulatto) might proudly proclaim, "I am a Negro American."

Following in this vein, I offer an amendment to Posnock's reading of the "madness" demonstrated by Du Bois, particularly his ill-conceived efforts in concert with Joel Spingarn to support and join the American forces during World War I, as well as his several serious missteps during his tenure at the NAACP. Posnock summarizes all of these "lapses" as Du Bois's self-conscious effort to denaturalize himself as a Black American, to produce himself as a quintessential cosmopolitan.

[H]is multiple strategies of denaturalization—the "Talented Tenth," the cult of distinction, aesthetic education, the flaunting of mulatto status, the ritual of choice to dramatize race as chosen rather than a biological given, and the construction of representation as troping rather than transparency—all work to turn race leadership from the eliciting of conformity and loyalty to the provocation to think and debate. (Posnock, 183)

Again I cannot say that I have any argument with the content of Posnock's reading of Du Bois's efforts. I do believe, however, that the process of denaturalization that Posnock narrates needs to be understood within its own historical contexts. Du Bois was able to make altogether logical pronouncements about choosing race and about his own mulatto status precisely because the mulatto was not for Du Bois or for his contemporaries simply a figurative element of their discourse. I have pointed out already that the mulatto category was not dropped from the census until 1920. Thus, for Du Bois in 1918, as for many others, the issue of denaturalization was not necessarily one that involved movement away from an already well-established black racial status, but instead one that represented movement toward a modern conception of racial distinction that did not always sit well with the black authors who are today thought to be some of its most significant proponents. More important, I believe that Du Bois's refusal to give up on what Anthony Appiah has called the "illusion of race" was not simply a matter of intellectual sloppiness but instead part of a larger movement among twentieth-century American intellectuals to open up the notion of Negro identity to the possibilities inherent in cosmopolitanism in a manner that was clearly not possible with (white) American identity.[4]

Jean Toomer is a particularly interesting figure in this regard. While I do not care to rehearse the now well-known details of Toomer's denial of black identity, I do want to dwell for just a moment on Posnock's treatment of the Toomer problematic. Specifically, I believe that Posnock is absolutely on the mark when he writes that Toomer was not, as many critics have suggested, simply uninterested in or bored by the question of race. He did not believe, like many contemporary scholars, that race is a false concept. Instead, Toomer's desire was for the production of a new race, an American race, one that would replace both the African and the European in the new world landscape. Thus, critics like Michael Lind celebrate Toomer not because he shows us the way toward an America in which we have given up on the fantasy of race but because he stands as a sort of founding father of a mixed, colored, mulatto America that is presumably in its ascendency.[5] I think it important to point out, however, that this notion of a mixed America predated Toomer and his contemporaries by at least a century. Black American authors of the nineteenth century were very much fascinated during various points of their careers with the possibility of America as a mulatto nation. There is also ample evidence to demonstrate that this notion of a mulatto, mestizo, culturally hybrid nation has been the norm in most of the other states of the new world, though by no means has this brought about an end to racism.

I return now to an argument that I made at the beginning of this essay, one that I believe may help in our understanding of the enigma of Jean Toomer as well as a number of other difficult Black American authors. I suggested earlier that during the

1920s much of the effort on the part of black writers was to erase the prior distinction that had once existed between the black and the mulatto. Specifically, I believe that the Harlem Renaissance might be properly understood as a moment when the production of modern American notions of racial distinctiveness rigidified. This process was helped along by whites, blacks, and even persons who once thought of themselves as mulatto in order to produce a stable black community, one that could be better exploited by industrial capital while simultaneously resisting that exploitation.

I ask, then, that we rethink what has become the standard reading of Du Bois's much quoted statement that "the world problem of the twentieth century is the problem of the color line." This statement, first made in the context of his address, in 1900, to the American Negro Academy, "The Present Outlook for the Dark Races of Mankind," is generally thought to be Du Bois's simple diagnosis of the reality of American racism. Wilson Moses, however, in his masterful reading of Du Bois's early development as an (Afrocentric) intellectual, seriously destabilizes the bases on which we might properly make this assumption. Moses expends considerable energy reproducing the intellectual peculiarities, if you will, of both Du Bois and the American Negro Academy. Specifically, he reminds us that Du Bois's thinking on race had been produced in response not simply to the everyday actualities of American society but, also and importantly, to the very specific intellectual influences of the other Academy members.[6]

Moses points to the fact that Du Bois's first speech in front of the Academy, three years earlier, titled "Conservation of Races" was essentially the young scholar's offering to his would-be mentor, Alexander Crummell, a figure with the moral and intellectual stature to stand between the looming personalities of Du Bois and Booker T. Washington, both of whom were invited to that first meeting. Crummell was noted for his cosmopolitanism (particularly his firsthand knowledge of various cultures of Europe, Africa, and America), as well as for his absolute commitment to racial solidarity. Thus, Moses reads "Conservation of Races" as specifically designed to quell concern that the assimilationist Du Bois was in line with the efforts and ideology of his peers.

Du Bois's Afrocentric rhapsody at the academy's first convocation was a manifesto for ethnic separatism and racial exceptionalism, and a call for enlightened despotism within a Pan-African culture. Du Bois presented the document as a "study-in-honor" of Crummell and as a declaration of solidarity with his racial ideals. The address celebrated ideas with which the senior black nationalist had long been associated: the firm belief in collective identity, the preachment of self-help, the unabashed advocacy of racialism. The ideas Du Bois expressed were closer to the spirit of Joseph de Maistre than of Thomas Jefferson, whose libertarian ideas it explicitly criticized. (Moses, 178)

If one continues with the line of argument offered by Moses, then it follows that we ought to consider whether Du Bois's color line statement was not simply diagnostic but perhaps didactic. Du Bois, the intellectual, the cosmopolitan, the mulatto, felt compelled, in that early stage of his development, to represent himself as a fellow traveler in the realm of Afrocentrism. Thus, when he proclaimed that the problem of the twentieth century would be the problem of *the* color line he was simultaneously gesturing toward the reality of white racism and disavowing competing ideas of race that could have—and indeed have—chipped away at the logical coherency of Afrocentrism. He did not proclaim that the problem of the twentieth century would be the problem of color lines, and in doing so he helped established himself—mulatto that he was—as the quintessential pan-Africanist.

Before I leave this point, I would like to dwell for a moment on the figure of William Ferris, Du Bois's contemporary and fellow participant at that first meeting of the American Negro Academy. Moses expends considerable energy examining the enigma that Ferris represents for Black American intellectual genealogies and arrives, I believe, at a point in his understanding of Ferris that has profound implications for contemporary American scholars. Ferris, like Du Bois, was among the first Black Americans to receive graduate degrees in this country (both received master's degrees from Harvard and Ferris received one from Yale as well). More important, he shared Du Bois's taste for aspects of high culture, and he was not at all squeamish about his rather pronounced elitism.

This would not be remarkable, in and of itself, if it were not for the fact that Ferris also wrote what is today considered a classic of Afrocentrism, *The African Abroad, or, His Evolution in Western Civilization, Tracing His Development Under Caucasian Milieu*, and that he joined Marcus Garvey's United Negro Improvement Association, eventually becoming a high-ranking official in that organization and a regular contributor to its newspaper, *Negro World*.[7] I do not mean at all to suggest that what is interesting about Ferris's story is that he somehow plunged from the heights of ivy-edged academia to the depths of street-corner Afrocentrism. Instead, what is compelling to me is the argument, advanced by Moses, that Ferris never relinquished either his elitism or his Eurocentrism, even as he became more and more deeply immersed in the development of an Afrocentric historiography. Specifically, Moses points to Ferris's extensive use of a variety of white authors on the subject of African history and culture, particularly Volney and Boas. And, while Ferris might be forgiven for this particular weakness by even the most stringent of contemporary Afrocentrists, it is simply impossible for anyone to escape the implications of Moses's claim that Ferris used his prominent position with several Black American newspapers, particularly *Negro World*, to inculcate within the black population not simply pride in their presumed Africanity but respect for the bourgeois values of white elites.

In fact, a figure like Ferris illustrates that black masses are receptive to the values of the white bourgeoisie. Ferris's work with several black newspapers enabled him to be a useful reinforcer of Anglo-American bourgeois values among the Afro-Americans who conceived themselves as being upwardly mobile. Particularly as literary editor of Negro World *during the 1920s, Ferris demonstrated the cosmopolitanism of Garveyism, and demonstrated that many of the cultural traits usually seen as the special province of educated elites were attractive to the black masses. (Moses, 189–190)*

As I have stated repeatedly, the strength of Moses's *Afrotopia* lies in his unwillingness to accept a clear distinction between Afrocentrism and cosmopolitanism. Instead, Moses radically refigures the genealogies of the two intellectual traditions so that they become largely indistinguishable. And, while he does not go quite as far as Posnock by explicitly stating that Afrocentrists were central figures in the initiation of discourses of cosmopolitanism in America, he clearly implies this in his work. Indeed, both authors expend much of their energies demonstrating that cosmopolitanism and Afrocentrism were always essentially interracial affairs, in terms of the identities of the traditions's proponents as well as of the social and political questions that they confront.

In the cases of William Ferris and W. E. B. Du Bois, Moses wastes no time in his efforts to demonstrate that their status as Afrocentric intellectuals was based on their deep immersion in the high cultural forms of western Europe and the United States. One of the more interesting connections between Moses's work and Posnock's, in fact, is that both make rather strong arguments for the centrality of Du Bois in the production of Afrocentrism and cosmopolitanism, respectively. I am suggesting here that the two works speak to each other with such resonance because, within the ideological structures of the subjects that they treat, Afrocentrism and cosmopolitanism, one finds a basic concern with the question of cross fertilization, hybridization, mixing, impurity. One always find the mulatto.

I have reiterated this simple point throughout my treatment of Posnock's and Moses's works because I believe that there is presently a profound lack of historical depth in what is sometimes referred to as race theory. Indeed, it comes to me always as somewhat of a shock to find American intellectuals celebrating interracialism as a peculiar phenomenon within our society. The truth is, of course, that the United States has had a very long tradition of racial intermingling, but this has not by any means guaranteed racial harmony. Moses himself points to the rather considerable efforts of (white) Charlotte Mason, particularly her patronage of Harlem Renaissance figures such as Alain Locke, Langston Hughes, and Zora Neale Hurston. The dollars that she provided for these luminaries and others came always with the expectation that they would celebrate the Africanity of their race, the primitivism of the Black American population, a primitivism that Mason understood as a corrective to the "artificial values" and "technological excess" that she attributed to Western culture.

It is telling that Mason was rewarded for her efforts with the title, "Godmother of the Harlem Renaissance." The image suggests the idea of an interracial family that nonetheless has escaped the funky taint of actual biological intermingling. Mason, the white mother, produces directly out of her head (or is it her purse?) putatively black children whom today we have absolutely no difficulty celebrating as the blackest of our black literary and cultural forbears.

Posnock and Moses led the way in moving us beyond an already stale set of debates by suggesting that what have been considered the most striking dichotomies in American cultural and intellectual life spring from exactly the same sources. Moreover, the great strength of both of their works stems from the fact that they disallow the notion that America is *becoming* a mulatto nation. Instead, *Color and Culture* and *Afrotopia* go a long way toward proving that America always has been a mulatto nation. My effort here is designed not to celebrate this reality but to ask whether the excitement with which some scholars approach the possibilities inherent in the hybrid, the mixed, the impure, and so forth is quite as well deserved as one might imagine. The idea that we are all somehow mixed is a notion with which any group of reasonably intelligent undergraduates will agree. The problem stems from the fact this agreement does little to change the actual conditions of living Americans. It does not guarantee that one develops a broad, intelligent, and engaged understanding of the greater world in which we live. Du Bois announced the color line as the great problem of the twentieth century because he understood the drawing together of all persons of African descent (black, mulatto, or some version thereof) as a strategic move in the progressive efforts to effect positive social change in the lives of millions of people. While I consider myself a fellow traveler in the efforts to dismantle this problem, to dismantle the color line, I must confess that I have heard and read little in this regard that actually reaches the level of social commitment, political engagement, and utopian vision that both Posnock and Moses rightly celebrate in the work of Du Bois. It is my great hope that in the twenty-first century many of us will take up the mantle thrown down by these authors and produce work that moves us beyond the veil and into the light of a bright American tomorrow.

III   At Home in America

Regarding this domestic issue, I must be the first to admit that I see that the black family unit is in ruins. It is our first and basic weakness. This fact may contribute much to our difficulty in uniting as a people. But for every effect there is a cause. If we are to understand and heal these effects we must understand the causes.

—GEORGE JACKSON, *Soledad Brother: The Prison Letters of George Jackson*

The belief that the black family, the black home, is in crisis, in ruins, has been one of the most palpable realities of U.S. culture. It has been bemoaned and pronounced upon by both black and white, from both the left and the right. It has been used as an argument for the erection of the welfare state—and for its dismantling—and it has been taken up as a subject of inquiry by a remarkably wide range of scholars and intellectuals. Indeed, the archive of the black family's demise is voluminous. From at least the mid-nineteenth century, American social commentators have been announcing the death of the black family and administering last rites. Still, we are reminded daily of the crisis, an obviously constant one (however counterintuitive that notion may be), one that somehow has become, I will argue, part of the basic vocabulary of America. Who are we? We are the nation in which the great, ruinous, ever eroding black family has been produced and produces. It is our first and basic weakness.

The work that I have set out for myself is to begin to produce a narrative of the discourse of black family crisis, particularly as it relates to the production of Black American radical thought of the sixties and seventies. In doing so, I will suggest that our eager willingness to announce the dilemma of the black family turns on our incredible reluctance to recognize not only the rather overdetermined nature of this discourse but, also and more important, the fact that the black family is a key site in the production of the *very* American notion of racial difference, the lie of America. What indeed constitutes the blackness of the black family, particularly the Black American family? The very question should startle the average American, given that we have moved only a step or two beyond rankly biological notions of racial identity such that one easily assumes that what she accesses when looking at my face is some corporeal history of Africa. Multiculturalism and our old-fashioned sympathies for mixed-raced persons aside, it is still quite possible to announce glibly the black family as *the* place in which Africans in America are nurtured and housed. To put the matter as plainly as possible, the black family allows us to do the difficult, expensive, and apparently quite necessary work of neatly and at a glance dividing up the descendants of slaves and the descendants of slave owners.

It is in precisely this sense that the black family represents a sort of necessary crisis for the generation of Black American radicals whom I invoke through the words of George Jackson. Jackson, jailed in 1960 and murdered by prison guards in 1970, wrote in that ten-year period hundreds of letters that, in the words of Jean Genet, demonstrate "the miracle of truth itself, the naked truth revealed,"[1] a truth that turned for Genet on an odd paradox in Jackson's life and work. George Jackson was at once the quintessential cosmopolitan *and* the absolutely self-limiting Black American. Genet hails Jackson as an intellectual cut from the same cloth as Sade, Artaud, and, of course, himself, then quickly, and with no apparent irony, remarks Jackson's racial difference. "Finally, every young American black who writes is trying to find himself and test himself, and sometimes, at the very center of his being, in his own heart, discovers, a white man he is trying to annihilate" (Genet, 338).

If one takes Genet at his word that the black intellectual is always at pains to annihilate the white man at the center of his being, then it follows that Jackson and other radical Black American intellectuals have had a rather severe conceptual problem with which to contend. Both Genet and Jackson imagine the black in America as a colonized subject. Genet tells us that Jackson writes in the "enemy's language," English. Meanwhile, Jackson struggles assiduously to reestablish access to an African ontology. "No other people have been completely divorced from their own as we have in such a short period. I don't even know my name." Again, the biologistic thinking of even the most radical of modern theorists continues to create a seamless unity between the West African captive of, say, the seventeenth century and the contemporary Black American. Rather, the only evidence that the black body gives in Jackson's narrative is evidence of Africa and enslavement, the evidence of one long, direct march through history, black body begetting black body.

My recall is nearly perfect, time has faded nothing. I recall the very first kidnap. I've lived through the passage, lain in the unmarked, shallow graves of the millions who fertilized the Amerikan soil with their corpses; cotton and corn growing out of my chest, "unto the third and fourth generation," the tenth, the hundredth.[2]

Let me not overstate the case that I am attempting to make here. I have no doubt that George Jackson and I are both the descendants of African captives and enslaved Americans. Moreover, I take quite seriously the moral imperative that we continue to honor the memory of these our ancestors by carrying on the struggle for justice, the struggle to end slave society. Still, I do not believe that what ties me to this past is a simple matter of biology. That is to say, if Jackson—as representative Black American—is able to reference some sort of racial memory that ties him to his enslaved ancestors, what is to stop him from accessing the memories of those who actually did the enslaving? He warns Angela Davis of his brother Jonathan, "Tell the brothers never to mention his green eyes and skin tone. He is very sensitive about it and he will either fight or withdraw."[3] These telltale green eyes and that never quite dark enough skin create a rather precise index of the traditions of racial commingling that exist more or less comfortably under the sign of blackness. The black in America has the maddening tendency to reveal in her eyes, skin, hair, in her body a history of contact and conquest, of slavery and rebellion, in which the African is certainly central, but never alone. Thus, when George Jackson nominates the black domestic unit as one of our basic weaknesses, when he argues that there are deep structures that produce these weakness, he begins to turn us, however awkwardly, toward serious consideration of the fact that the black family is perhaps not quite so black as we might imagine. The work of the black family is precisely to enable the maintenance of a coherent structure of American racialism. Blacks, browns, yellows, reds, and whites are given in black families access to a black body, the original body stolen from Africa, the innocent body, the body imagined as the site of revolution.

But Then There's Mama

It always starts with Mama, mine loved me. As testimony of her love, and her fear for the fate of a man-child all slave mothers hold, she attempted to press, hide, push, capture me in the womb. The conflicts and contradictions that will follow me to the tomb started right there in the womb. The feeling of being captured . . . this slave can never adjust to it, it's a thing that I just don't favor, then, now, never. (Jackson, 4)

I am certainly not the first to recognize that one of the most often executed maneuvers in the production and reproduction of discourses of black family crisis is the articulation of a strange, even uncanny, hostility to black women, a hostility that seems to turn precisely on black women's reproductive abilities, their fecundity, their promiscuity. I was brought back to this line of thinking, one that I have for a time now thought of as rather old-fashioned, after reading Charlotte Pierce-Baker's account of the rapes that she suffered in her home at the hands of two black male intruders. In the course of her narration of the trauma, Pierce-Baker comes close to asking whether the rape, the violence, was not itself an attack on her role as black mother, on her ability to take a black husband, produce a black child, create a black home.

When we bought the blue house, it was our dream house, made of old stone, surrounded by beautiful mature trees, a good neighborhood for children, in a multiracial area. But since the rapes, I realized and accepted that I would never again be able to live in a racially mixed or predominantly black neigh-borhood. The realization frightened and saddened me. I had been betrayed by my own people. I no longer had choices. Black men had raped and hu-miliated me. How could they do that to one of their "own"*? And so a different kind of lie crystalized—a lie of omission. I had to keep the rape a secret—I had a responsibility. But to whom? For what? Almost as if the crime had been perpetrated by someone I trusted.* That night one of the men had whispered, "You don't want your husband to know—do you?" I had replied, "Oh no."[4]

I want to attempt to index what that man, that black man, thought he was encouraging Pierce-Baker to hide, what she in-deed did hide. Of course, there were the actual acts that he was forcing Pierce-Baker to perform. But Pierce-Baker herself sug-gests that the rapists understood themselves as accessing some-thing other than her body. Rather, they accessed through her body some "prior responsibility" that preceded their onslaught. Pierce-Baker had a responsibility to the race, a mother's respon-sibility to not tell, to maintain a fiction of black unity. Pierce-Baker asks, "How could they do this to one of their own?" The question's challenge rests in the supposition that the men who attacked her did so not in spite of the fact that she was a black woman, a black mother, but because of that fact. Her husband, her child, her home, her successful (black) life are taken as evi-dence of a sort of a prior responsibility, proof that the black mother has given herself away to a sullied domesticity, an American concubinage. "You don't want your husband to know—do you?"

I remind my readers that as early as 1971 Angela Davis suggested that within some precincts of the Black American imaginary the enslaved woman is understood to be treacherous precisely because of her centrality to the reproduction and maintenance of the slave family.[5] What strikes me as odd is how little has been done to advance this line of argumentation. It seems that in the thirty years since the publication of Davis's article, many otherwise quite skeptical critics have come to accept the notion of not only a constant misogyny embedded within Black American radicalism but also the inevitability of that misogyny. The black man who, like George Jackson, expresses all manner of hostility to black women is taken to be either old-fashioned or perhaps so oppressed himself as to be "understandably" hostile to those closest to him.

Again, however, I reiterate my contention that the very longevity of the idea of black misogyny and our rather uncomplicated response to the same suggests the essentially ideological nature of the concept. The bad black mother does important work in the maintenance of the black community. She is the figure who takes up the management of the crisis that is the black family. She creates a home in America. She turns us black. Thus, she redirects, misdirects, our noble march back to Africa.

In the civilized societies the women do light work, bear children, and lend purpose to the man's existence. They train children in the ways of wisdom that history has shown to be correct. Their job is to train the children in their early life to be men and women, not confused psychotics! This is a big job, to train and propagate the race!! Is this not enough? The rest is left to the me: government administration, the providing of means of subsistence, and defense, or maintenance of life and property against any who would deprive us of it, as the barbarian has and is still attempting to do. The white theory of the "emancipated woman" is a false idea. You will find it, as they are finding it, the factor *in the breakdown of the family unit. (Jackson, 48)*

Jackson's narration of separate spheres ideology is incredibly precise. Women do light work, bear children, lend purpose to men's existence, and, most particularly, train and propagate the race. Men participate in business, government, and defense. Women are in the home, men are in the public world. The white theory of the "emancipated woman" is to be rejected.

The paradox is that at the very moment at which Jackson was imagining a black world with an essentially cloistered female population, the reality was that black women were entering in unprecedented numbers precisely the institutions that Jackson was hailing as exclusively male. As Jackson expressed his rage, his revolutionary ardor, inside increasingly small jail cells, female lawyers pressed his case, female activists kept his name before the public, and a handful of celebrity radicals: Angela Davis, Betty Shabazz, Kathleen Cleaver, Elaine Brown were left with the mantle of Black radicalism as the men in whose shadows they had once stood either died or ran. The truth for Jackson was that, at the very moment at which American society, particularly the American government, was intent upon destroying a variety of black radical organizations, one individual at a time, it was nonetheless embracing increasingly large segments of the communities that had spawned them. For Jackson, then, the much touted social, cultural, and economic boom of the post–World War II Black American community turned on the severing of that community's radical elements. The black community's domestication came at the expense of what was most radical, most black within it.

I think that it would be useful at this point to invoke the rather perplexing case of Frantz Fanon and his own difficult relationship to the question of blackness and Americaness, a relationship that

I will argue is mediated through Fanon's hostility to the productive black female, the bad black mother. Fanon demonstrates incredible sensitivity to the crisis of black domesticity, a crisis that for both Fanon and Jackson is enacted precisely at the site of the black female body. Fanon's intense hostility to Mayotte Capécia's novel, *Je suis Martiniquaise*, published in 1948, turns on his distaste for the black heroine's desire to take the white colonizer as her lover and thus, I argue, to produce through one presumably African and another supposedly European body an American, a creature whose skin bears the marks of respective black and white old worlds but whose origins are unquestionably within the new. Fanon writes:

One day a woman named Mayotte Capécia, obeying a motivation whose elements are difficult to detect, sat down to write 202 pages—her life—in which the most ridiculous ideas proliferated at random. The enthusiastic reception that greeted this book in certain circles forces us to analyze it. For me, all circumlocution is impossible: Je suis Martinquaise *is cut-rate merchandise, a sermon in praise of corruption.*[6]

We see that from the first moment at which he takes up Capécia's dirty little book, those two hundred two pages of pure corruption, Fanon is intent upon *not* reading it, refusing at all to recognize it as a piece of imaginative literature but instead seeing it as the very story of Mayotte Capécia, or rather, the perverse story of her corrupted (racialized) psyche.

Fanon is unwilling to recognize Capécia as his intellectual peer, a woman intent upon intervening in the ideological structures that hold together the lie of racial difference. Instead, his task in relation to Capécia is a simple one. He has but to construct her has an aberrant (black) creature, an ill, hysterical woman, a bad mama, such that her book does not become the site of a reasoned set of demands but instead becomes the place at which the evidence of the demeaning psychological effects of racism become apparent. He continues:

Mayotte loves a white man to whom she submits in everything. He is her lord. She asks nothing, except a bit of whiteness in her life. When she tries to determine in her own mind whether the man is handsome or ugly, she writes, "All I know is that he had blue eyes, blond hair, and a light skin, and that I loved him." It is not difficult to see that a rearrangement of these elements in their proper hierarchy would produce something of this order: "I loved him because he had blue eyes, blond hair, and a light skin." (Fanon, 43)

Fanon articulates only the notion that Capécia desired a white man *because of* his whiteness. Moreover, as I argued earlier, he insists that the work is not fiction but instead the actual narrative of the confused psyche of Capécia, a (black) psyche caught up in an always suspect desire for whiteness. Thus, there is only one way of reading *Je suis Martiniquaise*, as a rather pathetic attempt to give aesthetic life to the stinking phenomenon of internalized racism.

Yet the novel did receive an enthusiastic reception within, we may presume, certain Carribean and European circles. It *was* read and understood. The logic of the statement "I love him *because* he is white. I wish to marry him *because* he is the colonizer" was not lost on all of Capécia's interlocutors. I suggest, in fact, that Fanon's hostility to the novel and, more important, his inability to read it, his reduction of the work to autobiography, stems not from some inherent inscrutability within it—or within Capécia, for that matter—but, on the contrary, from the necessity of refusing to understand black disloyalty to blackness. If Fanon allows himself to read Capécia, then he will be forced to read through her a rather well-developed tradition of racial thought in which the Black American is understood not as a final product but, instead, as a means of becoming, a nodal point in the production of the American.

I remind my readers of the fact that the notion that black and white parents produce black children is a rather peculiar intellectual habit of the United States. Indeed, as Doris Sommer, Nick Shumway, Vera Kutzinski, and others have shown, the national romances of what we euphemistically call Latin America but which we might as easily refer to as colored America very often imagine the nation's genesis as precisely the coming together of the white colonizer, the native, and the black, the production of mulatto and mestizo culture.[7] In making this move, then, Capécia bluntly assaults what I call the notion of a Black American innocence, Black American exceptionalism. She disrupts the easy assumption of absolute unity between the black and the African, an assumption that always disallows the notion of the Black as *essentially* American, as the embodied site of American articulation. If Capécia does express a simple desire for whiteness, for the possession of power in flesh, then she does so not because of her irrationality but instead because she is infinitely rational, because she understands that whiteness marks the ugly—if strangely alluring—center. Rather, when the black woman possesses the body of the white man, when she bears his child, she challenges possession of the center, the very metropolis itself, she takes the chance that a black, a brown, a red, a yellow, a new subject formed within her own body, might take hold on the reigns of power, might displace the white father from his seat of victory.

The idea of racial mixing as a solution to the problem of white supremacy in the United States, not to mention the problem of an American republicanism sewn together with the threads of a seemingly insurmountable racial difference, *was* expressed by Black American intellectuals in both the nineteenth and twentieth centuries. I argue elsewhere that the difficulty that early Black American works like *Clotel, Our Nig,* and Phillis Wheatley's *Poems* pose for contemporary critics is that they are not particularly concerned to express a Black American specificity but instead are about the project of representing a real alternative (the mulatto, the yellow, the altogether deracialized) to increasingly rigid narratives of black/white difference.[8]

But then there's mama. Mama never likes it when we fight. Mama would rather build a home than burn one down, and she will not, cannot forget the names of her children, the names of their fathers. She is at once the link to Africa and the proof that there is no link. Mama disallows the possibility of escape more surely than any American jailer. In Haile Gerima's 1972 film, *Bush Mama,* the main character, Dorothy, poor, black, female, constantly moving and never getting anywhere, comes to the moment of violence, the moment of revolutionary articulation only after her husband, T.C., has been imprisoned and her child has been viciously raped by a white policeman. She is actualized, she becomes the romanticized bush mama, carrying a child in one hand and a gun in the other, only after she has failed in her domestic endeavors. In fact, Gerima is very careful to demonstrate a negative correlation between the domestic spaces that he establishes (the welfare office, the small, dingy apartment in which the rape takes place, the neighborhood bar) and the prison spaces in which both Dorothy and T.C. come to radical consciousness. The transparency of the prison, its very starkness, its refusal of the lie that the black is at home in America and is thus not a colonized subject, makes it infinitely more useful in the production of black radical subjectivity than the complicated space of the home.

Likewise, Gerima, himself referencing Fanon, understands violence as inevitable and perhaps necessary for the colonized subject engaged in the liberation of her mind and community. The entire generation of black radicals had immediately available to them, of course, the powerful example of the Viet Cong's resistance to the American military, very often in the person of the Black American soldier. T.C.'s flashbacks to horrors he had seen and committed in Vietnam work to remind us that the Black American has immediate access to a crystal-clear understanding of both America's shocking viciousness and its incredible vulnerability.

Following from this, I turn again to George Jackson's letters and particularly to the depth of hostility expressed within them toward Jackson's own mother, Georgia, hostility that is relatively absent in his dealings (literary and otherwise) with the rest of his family and associates. Jackson writes:

Black mama, you're going to have to stop making cowards: "Be a good boy"; "you're going to worry me to death, boy"; "Don't trust those niggers"; "Stop letting those bad niggers lead you around, boy"; make you a dollar, boy." Black Mama, your overriding concern with the survival of our sons is mistaken if it is survival at the cost of their manhood. (Jackson, 250)

In my reading of Jackson I have been struck not so much by the hostility that he demonstrates in relation to his mother as by his anxiety, his inability to narrate adequately her subject position. She is a failure, and yet she is charged with being all controlling.

She enjoys being tyrannized, yet she yearns for the comforts of the bourgeois. She is deeply conservative, and yet revolution cannot come except through her. It seems that if in Jackson's world the Black American "has a momentous historical role to act out," one for which "the whole world for all time in the future will love us and remember us as the righteous people who made it possible for the world to live on," then black mothers will have to be willing to make the ultimate sacrifice. They will have to raise their children, educate them, train them as strong, conscious black soldiers precisely so that they might strike at the heart of the beast—the beast within—and be slaughtered in turn.

On August 7, 1970, George Jackson's seventeen-year-old brother, Jonathan, raided the Marin County, California, courthouse, during the trial of three black inmates from San Quentin. He gave weapons to the inmates, then left with them and five hostages, including the judge. He demanded that his brother and the two other inmates, collectively known as the Soledad Brothers, be released immediately. He was dead within hours. Two days later George Jackson wrote:

Go over all the letters I've sent you, any reference to Georgia being less than a perfect revolutionary's mama must be removed. Do it now! I want no possibility of anyone misunderstanding her as I did. She didn't cry a tear. She is, as I am, very proud. She read two things into his rage, love and loyalty. (Jackson, 329)

It would be only a brief while before a guard on a gun tower shot George Jackson to death. Thus, we have the production of the perfect revolutionary mother, the mother who, as in Gerima's *Bush Mama,* has no sons.

Jackson's contemporary, Malcolm Little, lost his father as a child and gave up his father's name as an adult. Yet he maintained a tortured relationship to his own mother, a mother who seemed to be always offering her son up as sacrifice. The very first words of his autobiography reveal both her revolutionary ardor and her insanity.

When my mother was pregnant with me, she told me later, a party of hooded Ku Klux Klan riders galloped up to our home in Omaha, Nebraska, one night. Surrounding the house, brandishing their shotguns and rifles, they shouted for my father to come out. My mother went to the front door and opened it. Standing where they could see her pregnant condition, she told them that she was alone with her three small children and that my father was away, preaching, in Milwaukee. The klansmen shouted threats and warnings at her that we had better get out of town because "the good Christian white people" were not going to stand for my father's "spreading trouble" among the "good" Negroes of Omaha with the "back to Africa" preachings of Marcus Garvey.[9]

The perversity of this moment, the twisted logic that has been lost on almost all the autobiography's commentators,[10] is the fact that this woman, this quintessential black revolutionary mother, a mother so bold, so enraged that she would use herself and her unborn child to shield the home constructed by her absent—if revolutionary—husband, was no black at all. Indeed, her skin was fair, her hair was straight. Her father *was* white, Malcolm informs us, and "her accent did not sound like a Negro's" (Malcolm X, 2). Malcolm attributes his own tawny complexion, in fact, to his mother's quite certain parentage, and he spent much of his life hating that part of himself—fair skin, red kinky hair, bright eyes— that he attributes to some long-ago rape of a Caribbean woman.

What I believe Malcolm misses, the quite obvious fact that is never taken up in the course of the narrative but that screams out in all the accounts that he provides of his mother, especially the reports of her insanity and her cruelty, is the fact that Malcolm's mother, the fair Mrs. Little, *became* black in her own lifetime. She chose blackness. Thus, in reading her actions, particularly her beatings of the son who most favored her, I suggest not simply that she was insane (as Fanon does with Capécia) but instead that she was expressing the incredible sense of vertigo that she must have felt upon picking up wholesale a peculiar set of U.S. racial protocols. She was taking her first awkward steps toward becoming that strange American monstrosity: the "white" mother giving birth to "black" children.

Thinking about it now, I feel definitely that just as my father favored me for being lighter than the other children, my mother gave me more hell for the same reason. She was very light herself but she favored the ones who were darker. Wilfred, I know was particularly her angel. I remember that she would tell me to get out of the house and "Let the sun shine on you so you can get some color." She went out of her way never to let me become afflicted with a sense of color-superiority. I am sure that she treated me this way partly because of how she came to be light herself. (Malcolm X, 7–8)

Though I may be accused of apostasy here, I will hazard to say that Malcolm's reading of his mother's actions is incorrect. He believes that she beat him because of the way in which his face reminds her of a rape that she did not herself experience, reminds her of the inevitability of her own degraded situation. I would like us to imagine, however, that her motivations were exactly opposite to this. She struck her bright son not because she was a black woman looking into the face of the oppressor but because she was a "white" woman making a decision to turn that son black, to give herself over to the strictures of American racialism in a manner that would necessarily doom her and her son to a life of oppression but that would also open up to them a world of promise. I suggest that she sent Malcolm into the sun, she forced color upon him, because she knew that there was greater promise in the black tomorrow than in the tomorrow guarded by strange men in white sheets.

I ask you to take seriously for just a moment the often repeated but rarely believed notion that the people who have come to be known as Black Americans are actually agents of history, that they have had some significant part in the production of the social and ideological structures through which they—we—live our lives and have not been simply the victims of biological determinism. I ask that we attempt to understand blackness not as a thing, carried about in the bodies of persons, but instead as a rather complex set of social and discursive processes. I ask that we see Black American identity as a choice, a choice enacted every day in our movement into and out of schools, religious institutions, homes, jobs, sexual practices and partners, political parties, and our varied affiliations. And I ask, finally, that we seek understanding of why a distinct community of persons would make that choice. Why, indeed, have Black Americans not allowed the demise of the black family, the site that I have nominated as a central if not *the* central location in the production of American racial difference and thus a primary site in the production of racial assault, *racism*? Why have we not given ourselves over to narratives of racial mixing as almost all of our closest neighbors have and as at least some of our "ancestors" suggested? Why do we remain black?

I have begun already to sketch an answer to this rather unwieldy question by unpacking Fanon's hostility to Capécia's rather shocking lack of innocence, her unwillingness to create a narrative that clearly ties the "black" body in Martinique to the "black" body in Africa. By doing so, Capécia seriously problematizes the ground on which one might produce a radical (American) social theory. If the dark face reflects not simply the slave but the slaver, then how are we to distinguish the torturer from her victims? I contend that this problem perplexed Fanon enough to necessitate his removal to Africa itself in order to reestablish himself in presumably intimate relation to African natives. The Fanon of *The Wretched of the Earth* and *A Dying Colonialism*, the Fanon who defends the veil in Algeria, is a man considerably less troubled by the intricacies of racial difference than the one we see represented in *Black Skin/White Masks*. In his later works he achieves stunning clarity, remarkable innocence. The line between the colonized and the colonizer is apparent, and the just man has but one course of action: to strike at the heart of the colonizer, to kill the white man in both one's land and one's mind.

The starving peasant, outside the class system, is the first among the exploited to discover that only violence pays. For him there is no compromise, no possible coming to terms; colonization and decolonization are simply a question of relative strength. The exploited man sees that his liberation implies the use of all means, and that of force first and foremost.[11]

It is telling that Fanon makes such an explicit break with both Marxist and Freudian narratives of subject formation, refusing to accept at all the understanding that the modern (revolutionary) subject is produced not in contradistinction to the oppressive and, indeed, deadly aspects of capitalist and colonial culture but instead as a sort of rearticulation of the same. Fanon turns to the peasant precisely because *he* exists outside class society and thus somehow prior to always sullied dialectics, already suspect triangulation. Fanon, even as he writes in French, even as he establishes himself against the various "European" intellectual traditions in which he has been so well trained, is at pains to produce, to choose, an original—and originary—philosophy of revolution, one as pure as the body of the African native.

While it is not possible for me to take up the matter fully here, I do believe that it is important to at least to ask, given the comments I have just made, whether we may be reading our intellectual genealogies in the wrong direction. The steady interest in the work of Fanon by Black American intellectuals since the publication of *Black Skin/White Masks* and the huge spike in interest with the publication of *The Wretched of the Earth* is a matter almost beyond comment. What I suggest, however, is that our eager, greedy reception of Fanon may have to do with his telling us a story that we are infinitely prepared to hear, indeed, one that the Black American has been telling herself for quite some time. The rejection in the United States of racial ambiguity, written most clearly into law in *Plessy v. Ferguson,* was not simply a social phenomenon that happened to the Black American community but instead one in which it participated actively.

As I observed earlier, from the 1850s forward the work of U.S.–based black intellectuals has been, at least in part, to jealously guard the gates to the black home, to create a narrative of blackness that is at once biologistic and somehow innocent, purely black. Thus, we have Harper, Du Bois, Chesnutt, Griggs, and Johnson announcing in the late nineteenth and early twentieth centuries the absorption of a formerly distinct group of mulattos into the Black American population so that, by the time of the so-called Harlem Renaissance, Larsen, Thurman, Toomer, Locke, and others were caught up in the question of how to rectify the supposed Africanity of the black community with the reality of its cosmopolitanism. Thus, the novel of passing, the novel in which one can be black without acting or looking black, took center stage. I suggest here simply that the idea of a racial continuity that would tie the fairest to the darkest is a component of Fanon's work that did not come out of thin air but that on the contrary, had been developing in the Americas for more than a century.[12]

George Jackson wrote near the end of his life that "We have known for a long time now that the black man is, from the start, natively, the guilty man" (Jackson, 339). I take these words as a talisman for the work that I believe stands before students of the revolution in thought that took place among Black Americans in the post–World War II era. Indeed, what I believe Jackson, Malcolm X, Frantz Fanon, and others came close to accessing at the close of their lives was not simply the fact that racial difference is chosen but also the reality that, in that choosing, Black American people long ago lost their innocence. The evidence of our guilt lies in the fact of our survival. There is still a Black American community; thus, there is all manner of unspeakable perversity that necessarily precedes and accompanies that community. The phrase "bad black mama" is a study in redundancy. She is, indeed, the figure who produces the revolutionary, then rushes to cool his ardor, his tendency toward self-destruction. As such, she is perhaps *the* key player in the management of the very American crisis of the black family. She is, therefore, a creature who readily provokes great reverence *and* icy hot hostility. The question that

I leave you with, then, is, What next? What lies beyond the black family and its constant production, however awkward, of black people, with their black problems and black crises? What is the nature of the choices available to those of us who yearn for a just society, for those of us at home in America?

GAY

IV Dinge

There is indeed a close interrelation between the predominant Western conception of manhood and that of racial (and species) domination. The notion, originally from myth and fable, is that the summit of masculinity—the "white hero"—achieves his manhood, first and foremost, by winning victory over the "dark beast" (or over the barbarian beasts of other—in some sense, "darker"—races, nations and social castes.)

> —PAUL HOCH, *White Hero, Black Beast: Racism, Sexism and the Mask of Masculinity*

If there is one thing that marks us as queer, a category that is somehow different, if not altogether distinct, from the heterosexual, then it is undoubtedly our relationships to the body, particularly the expansive ways in which we utilize and combine vaginas, penises, breasts, buttocks, hands, arms, feet, stomachs, mouths and tongues in our expressions of not only intimacy, love, and lust but also and importantly shame, contempt, despair, and hate. Because it is impossible to forget that we hold a tangential relationship to what Michael Warner calls heteronormativity, we often are forced to become relatively self-aware about what we are doing when we fuck, suck, go down, go in, get on, go under. Even and especially when I encounter the nameless trick, even and especially when that tricking happens in the blank, barely penetrable atmosphere of the dark room, I am aware of the immense contradictions at play, the pleasure and the danger located at the end of his cock, pleasure and danger that are intimately linked and that work together to produce the electricity of the encounter. Essex Hemphill writes, "Now we think as we fuck. This nut might kill. This kiss could turn to stone."[1]

It is surprising, then, that so little within queer theory has been addressed to the question of how we inhabit our various bodies, especially how we fuck or, rather, what we think when we fuck. In the face of wildly impressive work on gay and lesbian history and historiography, gender roles and politics, queer literature and culture, we have been willing to let stand the most tired and hackneyed notions of what our sex actually means. If you believe the propaganda, it would seem that every time a fag or dyke fingers a vagina or asshole is a demonstration of queer love and community. The exceptions to this rule come almost invariably from what we might think of as the queer margins. Sadomasochistic practice and the debates surrounding it, particularly among lesbians, reminded us that dominance, submission, and violence, real or imagined, are often integral parts of queer sexual practice. The H.I.V./A.I.D.S. community helped focus our thinking about issues of risk, disease, and decay. Further, and more importantly for my purposes here, nearly two decades of writing and film making by people of color, and in particular the work of black gay men, has spoken to the experience of sex with whites, painting it at once as liberatory and repressive.

It is telling that cultural practitioners as distinct as Marlon Riggs, Isaac Julien, and Lyle Harris all found it necessary to identify themselves as snow queens, or some version thereof, in recent years. Indeed, the articulation of a persistent, if diffuse and diverse, black hunger for vanilla has been such a regular aspect of the various discussions of black subjectivities as to seem rather mundane. In 1853, William Wells Brown published the first Black American novel, *Clotel*, in which his near-white female protagonist is first seduced, then abandoned by a handsome young planter. Wallace Thurman continued the theme more than seventy years later as he explored the tension generated by thinly veiled interracial and homosexual desire in his *Infants of the Spring*, tension that is relieved for the white protagonist within the vaginas of several readily available black women and for the black in an ascetic devotion to his art.[2] In the fifties and sixties, Eldridge Cleaver, Piri Thomas, and Malcolm X all confessed their dalliances on the other side of the line, their moments in the sun. Indeed, black queers as diverse as James Baldwin, Audre Lorde, Samuel Delany, and Essex Hemphill have all paid considerable attention to the questions engendered when one "sleeps with the enemy."

What is striking, given the tradition that I have just outlined, is the fact that so few white artists, critics, intellectuals of all stripes, male or female, lesbian or gay, have found it necessary to cover themselves in the mantle of dinge queen, rice queen, or what have you. The desire for black, brown, and yellow flesh remains largely unspoken within either academia, or even within popular publishing. Not since the mid-eighties and the release by Gay Sunshine Press of *Black Men/White Men* have I seen a sustained articulation of cross-racial desire by any white person, though the evidence from the personal ads, the 900 lines, and the porn magazines suggests that dark meat is in exceptionally high demand as we enter the new millennium.[3]

I am not attempting to further police queer sexuality, to suggest that cross-racial desire and fantasy is necessarily a bad or shameful thing. On the contrary, I am enough a product of the "liberal" seventies to imagine that when black dick meets white dick we all are one step closer to the beloved community. Still, the question remains, What do we think when we fuck? Why is it that we often find such sustained discussions of cross-racial desire among people of color, while whites remain largely silent? My attempt to answer this question turns largely on the work that is just beginning to emerge from a variety of scholars in which whiteness is named as a reality, or more accurately, as an ideological structure that stands not so much in contradistinction to blackness, or Latinoness, or Asianness, but in intimate relation to them. David Roediger opens his study of white ethnicity and class consciousness, *The Wages of Whiteness*, with a discussion of the highly overdetermined manner in which stereotypes of black bodies and desires affect white sexuality. Increasing numbers of critics, among them Alexander Saxton, Richard Dyer, Toni Morrison, and Eric Lott, are attempting to open up our understandings of white subjectivity to demonstrate how blackness is indeed the always already lurking in the netherworld of white consciousness.[4] Significantly, each of these scholars has suggested that this reality, the blackness of whiteness, is denied precisely because whiteness itself has been rendered transparent. Whiteness seems incapable of recognizing itself until it is put under extreme pressure, until it is confronted with the hypervisibility of blackness. My contribution to these discussions is to argue that sexuality, no, let me say fucking, is one of the primary nodes at which this process of blackness into whiteness takes place. I contend, in fact, that the tendency to insist upon the innocence of our sex, the transparency of desire at the moment of penetration, is itself part of the complex ideological process by which whiteness is rendered invisible, unremarkable except in the presence of a spectacularized blackness.

At the Connection in Berlin, I am accosted by a drunk, white American expatriate. He badgers me and my companions: a six-foot-four, 225 pound dark-skinned psychologist and a small, light brown broker, complaining that he cannot attract the attention of the blond Aryan types that he desires because they are overly interested in us. I counter that just beyond our group there is a door that leads to a maze-like backroom in which dozens of men are literally begging to be taken by dark-haired, moderately developed, white thirty-five-year-olds. He persists, pointing to the German fascination with the exotic and the relative ease this affords blacks, particularly Black Americans, in the sexual economy. I remind him that I am from the suburbs and then tell a story about waiting for a bus in Alexanderplatz and people reaching out to touch my skin and hair, at first gingerly, discreetly, and then with passion, eventually forcing me to break away to the other side of the street. I tell him that a few days earlier an East German scared me when he overtook me on the sidewalk, barred my path, insisted on knowing who I was, then begged me to meet him again while friends gruffly pushed him aside and pulled me away. In his stupor, a stupor imported all the way from America, my friend cannot hear me. Mercifully, he leaves, surfacing hours later with a cache of backroom war stories and a huge smudge on his forehead made from the iridescent ink stamped onto the backs of our hands as we entered the club. Even then, I was struck by the irony that this mark of his transgression, this sign of his desirability, of fully inhabiting a clearly raced and gendered body, was visible only under the black light.

What strikes me now in listening to myself relate this episode is not simply how omnipresent racism is within the lives of blacks and other people of color. That is old news. Nor am I attempting to deny the heightened ability of Black American gay men to participate in a sort of cross-racial sexual tourism outside U.S. boundaries. I am not even particularly surprised at how threatened some whites, many whites, most whites are at the spectacle of the visible black, the beautiful black, the black who is desired. What is really stunning, however, is the honesty and clarity with which this man expressed what I take to be a rather profound alienation from his own corporeality, his so-called whiteness, alienation that is focused and transmitted precisely through racist discourse. Upon consideration, what seems to have been taking place, within a sexually tense leather bar in a Germany that always is understood as wildly racist and anti-Semitic, was a breakdown of the very ideological structures by which we construct our various identities: racial, national, sexual, what have you. We were both out of bounds, existing as anomalies in language and culture, freaks to be either exoticized or pitied. My interlocutor seems to have been thrashing about in a fit of anxiety engendered by his will to recapture normality in the face of the intense sense of vertigo that we shared. Strangely enough, I, with all my familiar bestial, intensely sexual blackness, was the only sign by which he seemed capable of reestablishing boundaries, of maintaining a self in the midst of constant erosion. Paul Hoch writes,

To abandon control over the bestial super-masculinity he has projected outward onto the black male would threaten the racist's control over his own repressed sexuality (which forms the basis for that projection), and over all the bestial niggers and rapists locked within his psyche who threaten to erupt in a mad orgy of sexual violence. The black man must therefore be "kept down," not to protect the white goddesses, but because on the sub-conscious level his liberation would signify the eruption of the sexuality con-fined in the racists's own unconscious, hence a catastrophic loss of his con-scious self, a "castration." (Hoch, 55–56)

I stress again the observation that I made earlier in this essay that the process by which the white male might abandon control over what Hoch calls "bestial super-masculinity" is one and the same with the process by which he might lose access to his whiteness. Moreover, the technology that mitigates against this procedure ever occurring is the very technology that renders whiteness transparent. When the black is seen, the white is not. Yet the workings of desire, the will to be recognized, taken, possessed, involves at least a temporary lapse in this invisibility. The black is necessary, then, as a sort of prosthetic, much like the fabricated outer skin manufactured by Orwell's own invisible man. Our presence gives the white form. But always there is the danger that the most sacrosanct boundaries might be crossed, that the man inside might cease to exist as an entity unto himself and become instead a breach, a break, a horrid violation of both self and other. "Now we think as we fuck. This nut might kill us. This kiss could turn to stone."

Interestingly enough, it is James Baldwin who has worked most assiduously to tell us what it is that white men, particularly white queer men, think when they fuck. Vivaldo, Eric, Yves, Giovanni, and David all struggle to speak their desire in the course of Baldwin's narratives. More important, the process by which they come to voice, *if* they come to voice, is always one and the same with the process by which they come to refuse the inevitability of an inarticulate whiteness. Indeed, I suggest that the difficulty that so many critics have when approaching Baldwin is precisely that they seem incapable of maintaining or even acknowledging his intense investment in understanding the manner in which white masculinity is codified in relation to "blackness," understood here as that almost otherworldly existence that is not white. Instead, the rather underdeveloped critical literature surrounding Baldwin tends to turn upon proving or disproving his allegiance to an ill-defined black aesthetic. One must remember always that Baldwin is *the* black author, the paragon of the Black American intellect, the nation's prophet of racial tolerance, one whose queer sexuality presumably stands in such anomalous relation to his racial presence, intellectual and otherwise, that it works only as the exception proving the rule.[5]

Part of the violence that is visited continuously upon Baldwin's work, the body of Baldwin, is a sort of collapsing of ontological and epistemological considerations. The black author thinks black. Baldwin seems, though, to always slip the yoke of his various identities, some self-imposed, others not. He refused, throughout his career, to accept the neat categories into which we deposit our multiple selves, preferring instead to insist upon the funkiness of our existences, or, more to the point, he forces us to consider the shocking manner in which what we think when we fuck is not so much dictated by race, gender, and class but instead acts itself as an articulation of the structures of dominance—and resistance—that create race, gender, and class. Baldwin writes:

The American ideal, then, of sexuality appears to be rooted in the American ideal of masculinity. This ideal has created cowboys and Indians, good guys and bad guys, punks and studs, tough guys and softies, butch and fag-

got, black and white. It is an ideal so paralytically infantile that it is virtually forbidden—as an unpatriotic act—that the American boy evolves into the complexity of manhood.[6]

The ideals that Baldwin points to are ones that are constructed through the erection and maintenance of a set of false, if potent, binarisms: good/bad, punk/stud, butch/fag, what have you. For Baldwin, though, the primary binarism, the model from which and through which he filters the presumably natural divisions in the human condition, is none other than the one that both holds together and separates the black and the white.

It is with these ideas in mind that I suggest that we begin to reread Baldwin's *Another Country*, particularly his depiction of the "optically white" Vivaldo. Baldwin so insists throughout the work on forcing consideration of the black/white binarism—white handkerchief in black hands, black tie on white shirt, white dick against black dick against black vagina against white vagina—that the distinctions clearly begin to crumble by the end of the narrative.

He stared into his cup, noting that black coffee was not black, but deep brown. Not many things in the world were really black, not even the night, not even the mines. And the light was not white, either, even the palest light held within itself some hint of its origins, in fire.[7]

That Italian Vivaldo, who comes from a Brooklyn neighborhood much like the Harlem onto which he has projected so many fantasies, is not "white" is far from being the tragedy of this work. On the contrary, the tragedy, the horror that both the white and the black subject must confront in Baldwin's universe, is the racial fantasy that denies access to the body, that denies access to the beloved, and instead seals each partner into a bizarre competition in which mutual invisibility is the inevitable outcome. Indeed, the "lovemaking" in *Another Country* is as much an act of rage and hate as of adoration and devotion.

The battle was awful because the girl wished to be awakened but was terrified of the unknown. Every movement that seemed to bring her closer to him, to bring them closer together, had its violent recoil, driving them farther apart. Both clung to a fantasy rather than to each other, tried to suck pleasure from the crannies of the mind, rather than surrender the secrets of the body. (Baldwin, Another Country, *131)*

Baldwin has clearly identified the catalytic tension in the labored give and take between the two partners, Vivaldo and Ida, the younger sister of Vivaldo's dead (black) friend, Rufus. Each wants to break, to move beyond identity, not to know, but to surrender to the secrets of the body. Yet their laboring, their performance of intimacy, works only to reconstruct difference. The two are most sealed in their blackness and their whiteness, "in full narcissistic cry," as Fanon would have it, at precisely the moment of their "joining."

And what of Rufus, the ghost who haunts even Vivaldo's most intimate interactions?

It is Rufus whom he tries to save. It is Rufus whom he constantly insists that he loves. It is Rufus whose lost life he carries about as a regretful and irrepressible memory. As Vivaldo fucks Ida, as Vivaldo hires a series of black prostitutes, as Vivaldo seduces/is seduced by Eric, a (white) gay man who is himself a "nigger lover," who himself has loved Rufus, he is haunted not only by remorse and regret at the tragedy suggested by his friend's life and death but by a certain half-acknowledged fear that he neither knew nor particularly loved this man around whom so much in his emotional and social economies was constructed. When confronted with Ida's angry and breathless claim to having loved her brother, Vivaldo responds: "'So did I' . . . too quickly, irrelevantly; and for the first time it occurred to him that, possibly, he was a liar; had never loved Rufus at all, but had only feared and envied him" (Baldwin, *Another Country,* 413).

Vivaldo's fear of Rufus is one and the same with his fear of knowledge. He is afraid to know not only that he never loved Rufus but that the barrier to that love was the very ideology of seamlessness, the insistence that he does not see difference, the "color-blindness," that dictates his relationships with not only Rufus and Ida but Eric, Cass, and her husband, Richard, as well. Rufus embodies not simply difference but, perhaps more important, the knowledge and acknowledgment of the processes through which difference is constructed. Rufus recognizes in his fucking, moreover, an incredible opportunity in which to express this knowledge.

He wanted her to remember him the longest day she lived. And, shortly, nothing could have stopped him, not the white God himself nor a lynch mob arriving on wings. Under his breath he cursed the milk-white bitch and groaned and rode his weapon between her thighs. She began to cry. I told you, *he moaned,* I'd give you something to cry about, *and at once, he felt himself strangling, about to explode or die. A moan and a curse tore through him while he beat her with all the strength he had and felt the venom shoot out of him, enough for a hundred black-white babies. (Baldwin,* Another Country, *22)*

Rufus abuses himself, abuses his white lovers, Leona and Eric, then throws his body off the George Washington Bridge. And yet he does not die. He lives always and especially with Vivaldo, who climbs in and out of bed with his lost friend, searching in the bodies of multiple surrogates for some part of himself that he imagines Rufus took with him into the waters of the Hudson.

Again I stress my contention that the difference that haunts Vivaldo is not some free-floating, omnipresent signifier, some pregiven reality. On the contrary, the difference that besets them all is a difference that is constructed—and reconstructed—precisely at those moments of intimate contact. It is almost as if the camp fiction of whiteness, the fiction of the white dick, is put on display at precisely the moment when it presumably is thrown aside. As Vivaldo struggles into the body of Ida, he does not simply find Rufus, or Eric, or any of the faces from his world of sexual experience. Instead, he finds some carnivalesque image of himself, a grotesquely white boy laughing at his feeble efforts to become a man. "It is an ideal so paralytically infantile that it is virtually forbidden—as an unpatriotic act—that the American boy evolves into the complexity of manhood."

It is important here that I guard against the assumption that what I am describing is *simply* a species of racial fetishism. Indeed, the question that I have asked—What do we think when we fuck?—has not been limited to those whites who fuck blacks but instead applies to the entirety of (white, Western, male) sexual desire. If Vivaldo cannot get the Negro off his mind as he fucks black women, the same is true of Eric as he fucks white men and women, of Richard as he fucks Cass, and of Ellis, Richard's business mentor, as he fucks everyone. One of my primary goals is to suggest that, even and especially in those most sacred moments of sexual normativity (white dominant male on white submissive female), the specter of the black beast is omnipresent. As the good white wife, Cass, goes home to tell her dutiful and faithful husband of her affair with the gay, race traitor, Eric, she pauses for a moment in the cab, exchanging glances with the young Puerto Rican driver, taking a moment to allow desire to wash over her before she faces the truth and the violence that she knows are inevitable.

Even now, even as we fuck, I smack your buttocks hard. No, not the slight licks that work only to remind us of the fullness of flesh. When I strike out I do mean to hurt, if only to catch your attention for a moment, to startle you with cruelty, to see you writhe on the bed, begging, "Please be gentle." And even so you forget me, disremember laughter and witty conversation about puppets and acting, lose the image of my face as dick passes into rectum. In the morning, no longer drunk, you cannot speak. I leave, your card in hand, scuttle to the subway, a little embarrassed, tired, still hungry.

What I have been concerned with, in these brief comments, is the question of silence. Why, I have asked, do we see so little work by white gays and lesbians that directly addresses the question of cross-racial desire? I have suggested that we might at least begin an answer by paying attention to the way in which speaking to these issues, admitting to the reality of beauty that is other than white, throws into disarray the idea of whiteness as universal. The point seems easy enough to understand. What is more difficult to accept is the idea that the sexual act, at least as it is performed between queers—and yes, I am nominating Vivaldo as queer—is not necessarily a good, expansive, and liberatory thing, a place in which individuals exist for a moment outside themselves such that new possibilities are at once imagined and actualized. This notion is itself predicated upon the articulation of a set of false boundaries, oddly constructed binarisms in which the black always comes up short. I am fully suspicious, in fact, of the notion of transcendence, of seamless, nonparticularistic connection with the rest of existence precisely because it looks so much like the imagined transparence that I have argued defines whiteness. We do not escape race and racism when we fuck. On the contrary, this fantasy of escape is precisely that which marks the sexual act as deeply implicated in the ideological processes by which difference is constructed and maintained. In Berlin there is a white man who cannot get his nut for fear that my black hand might have caressed the flesh of the blond and blue *ubermensch* he so desires. In Baldwin's *Another Country*, Vivaldo cannot connect, cannot come because he is so busy fooling himself that he exists outside his body, in a terrain in which love and desire conquer all.

The task that awaits all of us, then, is to speak desire plainly, to pay attention to what we think when we fuck. It is the particular task of white men to give up the comforts of naivete, of banal gestures to racial inclusion. The work before us is precisely to put our own bodies on the line. We must refuse to allow the production of a queer theory so reified that it does nothing to challenge the way we interact, the way we think, and the way we fuck. We must insist on a queer theory that takes the queer body and what we do with it as a primary focus, lest we allow for the articulation of a queer subjectivity that never recognizes the differences we create and carry in our bodies, including not only race but gender, health, and age, to name only the most obvious categories. We must not only think as we fuck but also pay close attention to all the implications, good and bad, of those sometimes startling thoughts.

V Tearing the Goat's Flesh

Thou shalt not seethe a kid in his mother's milk.

—Exodus 23:19

Chivo que rompe tambor con su pellejo paga.

—Abakua proverb

Prologue, or De-Queering Robert Reid-Pharr

I would like to take a few moments to share with you the rather
pedestrian publication history of the essay you are about to read.
I began it in the early 1990s as a chapter of my dissertation and
designed it, like all too many final chapters of apprentice works,
as an update of what I thought of as my decidedly unsexy struggles to rework some hackneyed notions about the ideological and
aesthetic origins of Black American literature. In particular, I
wanted to demonstrate the salience of anxieties around masculinity in the production and reproduction of narratives of Black
American nationality. I failed. Rather, the work became the occa-
sion for the awkward mumblings and nervous twitchings of
members of my dissertation committee. They all generally agreed
that the piece had some merit but did not do the work that I had
intended it to do. It did not help better theorize the question of
Black American originality. Though they did not say so at the

time, my sense now is that those quite responsible and careful scholars feared that I had attempted in that final chapter to slip in, more or less illegitimately, some not yet well considered version of queer studies in the same way that graduate students today continue the sad comedy of inserting "race" chapters into otherwise "lily white" dissertations.

The fear was borne out when, during my first-ever job interview, a well-known scholar of postcolonial literature asked me whether my work was on Black American literature or queer theory. My reaction to her question was much like my reaction to the lingering smell of the cigarettes she had just smoked. I thought that it was not exactly improper but certainly not polite. The situation was made worse by the fact that I offered a completely underwhelming response to her, one based in the reality that I was not at all certain what queer theory was and indeed had no real memory of having heard the term before that day. Needless to say, I did not get the job, nor did I include the chapter in the book that eventually grew out of my dissertation.

Still, I am nothing if not an ambitious person and a quick study. I availed myself in due time of the work of many of the most significant queer theorists, some of whom I had been reading for years in other contexts. I also continued to pursue publication opportunities in both academic and popular media. More to the point, I continued to look for a home for my purportedly queer essay. I eventually found it, unremarkably enough, in a special issue of the journal *Studies in the Novel*. I had "queered" the work significantly in the intervening years, encasing it in what I took to be the latest and most sophisticated developments within the field. I had done so not so much because I was eager to develop a reputation as an up-and-coming theorist but because I understood that "queer" marked a promising site on which to peddle my intellectual wares. I had begun to understand queer theory not so much as a set of theoretical problems to be confronted or maneuvered but instead as an institutional apparatus. I recognized that I was receiving many more invitations to speak at queer events, to appear on queer panels, to comment on queer papers, than to demonstrate my expertise in (Black) American literature and culture. Thus, as the saying goes, "as all roads lead north, I headed north."

I sent a draft of the piece to the editor of the special issue, Eve Sedgwick, who gave me a set of extremely useful comments that I quickly incorporated. Things then proceeded more or less smoothly until she contacted me sometime later to say that the editor of the journal had objected to much of the language in the essay. I had used the words "cock," "pussy," and "fuck" too often for his tastes, and my work threatened, he argued, the relationship of the journal to the university and the state legislature. I became hot, then cold, then hot again but finally conceded to some of his demands, deleting a cock here, a pussy there, and throwing up scare quotes around the odd "motherfucker." I continued, however, to be amazed by the implication that, even though utilizing a queer apparatus implied a commitment to bringing new topics into polite academic discourse, it did not obligate one to call into question the necessity of the polite, civil, gentlemanly nature of that discourse. I also felt strongly that the editor had (dis)missed the fact that much of the essay is concerned with returning us to an understanding that black and gay identities have been creatively crafted out of the basest of insults. And, while this is indeed reason for celebration, this does not diminish the fact that a hint of that reality, our origins in the never-never world of niggers, coons, punks, faggots, and maricones is apparent in even the most positive articulations of race and sexuality.

Still, the essay *was* eventually printed and then reprinted in a collection also edited by Sedgwick, *Novel Gazing*. It has recently been published again in a collection of African American Literary Theory, alongside the work of some stellar contemporary critics: Houston Baker, Hortense Spillers, Wahneema Lubiano, Hazel Carby, Phillip Brian Harper, as well as several giants of Black American literary and cultural thought: Alain Locke, Richard Wright, W. E. B. Du Bois, Ralph Ellison, Amiri Baraka. The editor of the collection, Winston Napier, establishes in his introduction and in the architecture of the work an incredibly pure genealogy between Black critics of the early twentieth century and those of us working at the beginnings of the twenty-first. I was surprised to find my now heavily overburdened essay included among the works of critics whom I respect and a few whom I revere. I was equally surprised to find that it was included precisely because it was "queer." Indeed, Napier names me as one of a growing body of "black queer theorists" and argues that "Tearing the Goat's Flesh" is a direct response to Charles Nero's call in his "Toward a Black Gay Aesthetic" for the development of a black queer theory. I was dumbfounded. I had the sense of being at once deeply honored and profoundly misread.

My relationship to the projects of producing either a queer or a black aesthetic is at best tentative, complicated, undecided. While I celebrate the work of black people, gay people, and black gay people in almost all of my writing, I remain particularly suspicious about the precious ways in which we hold onto our old identities and fashion new ones out of them. I still have to resist the impulse to flinch when someone refers to me as a queer and to positively run for cover when someone refers to me as a black queer, as I have not yet rid myself of the suspicion, left over from my childhood, that I am being politely hailed as a nigger and a faggot. My interest in queer theory, and indeed all the theoretical apparatuses from which I have borrowed, stems not from an interest in producing positive images of black gays and lesbians. Instead, I am more concerned to mark the incredible slippage in meaning that necessarily accompanies even the most progressive articulations of modern identity. You say black gay. I hear nigger fag. "Tearing the Goat's Flesh" is best understood, then, not as evidence of a burgeoning black queer theory but instead as an effort on my part to affect the corrosion of the easy manner in which we talk about all identities, to demonstrate the funky, messy underside of the brave new world that some of us hope to fashion.

I argue in this work that the black gay stands in for the border crossing and boundarylessness that has so preoccupied contemporary Black American intellectuals. In particular, I argue that black gay men represent in modern American literature the reality that there is no normal blackness, no normal masculinity to which the black subject, American or otherwise, might refer. Indeed, Orlando Patterson, Henry Louis Gates, and Paul Gilroy, among others, have argued that the black has been conceptualized in modern (slave) culture as an inchoate, irrational nonsubject, as the chaos that both defines and threatens the borders of logic, individuality, basic subjectivity.[1] In that schema, all blacks become interchangeable, creating among the population a sort of continual restlessness, a terror.

I would add to this that antihomosexual violence operates in the production of black masculinity on two levels. First, the strike against the homosexual acts as a seemingly direct confrontation with the presumption of black boundarylessness, or we might say the assumption of black subhumanity and black irrationality that has its roots deep in the history of slavery and the concomitant will to produce Africans as "Other." To strike the homosexual, the scapegoat, the sign of chaos and crisis, is to return the community to normality, to create boundaries around blackness, rights that white men are obliged to recognize.

Second, and perhaps more important, this violence allows for a reconnection to the very figure of boundarylessness that the assailant is presumably attempting to escape. As a consequence, black subjects are able to transcend, if only for a moment, the very strictures of normality and rationality that have been defined in contradistinction to a necessarily amorphous blackness. To put it bluntly, we must empty our consciousness of that which is contradictory and ambiguous and most especially that which disallows our differentiation. Still, we seem not to be able to complete this process. We become uncomfortable with "realness" at precisely those moments when it appears to be most firmly established. Even as the profligate subject is destroyed, we retain "him" within the national consciousness, always on the brink of renewal, lest we find ourselves entrapped within a logic of subjectivity from which the black is excluded already.

I

The formal and rhetorical strategies that link Eldridge Cleaver's *Soul On Ice*, James Baldwin's *Giovanni's Room,* and Piri Thomas's *Down These Mean Streets* are not immediately apparent. Cleaver's and Thomas's texts are "autobiographical" and analytical, while Baldwin's is fictional. Cleaver documents what has become one of the most recognizable, one might even say trite, markers of black masculinity, incarceration, while both Thomas and Baldwin attempt to push against the confines of American blackness altogether. Thomas charts the difficulty that a young, dark-skinned Puerto Rican encounters as he tries to make sense of an American racial economy that creates him as "black," while Baldwin opts to step outside the confines of American race literature altogether, producing a novel in which there are no black characters but, as I argue later, in which race is one of the central signifiers.

At the same time, there is the pressing question of how we are to read Baldwin's "gay" novel in relation to the virulent homophobia of Eldridge Cleaver, a homophobia that reaches its apex at precisely those moments when it is directed specifically at Baldwin and his work, particularly *Another Country*. A similar question surrounds the work of Piri Thomas, whose antigay sentiment is just as apparent as, if somewhat less virulent than, Cleaver's. One might argue, in fact, that Cleaver, Thomas, and Baldwin belong to distinct literary camps such that any attempt to read the three together can proceed only by pointing out the variety of the diametric oppositions. Still, as Paul Gilroy has suggested in a discussion of John Singleton's *Boys in the 'Hood* and Marlon Riggs's *Tongues Untied,* even as the black neomasculinist heterosexual attempts to distance himself from homosexuality, he draws attention to the "similarities and convergences in the way that love between men is the common factor. . . ."[2] It follows that the key to understanding the depth of Thomas's and Cleaver's homophobia lies precisely in the fact that the universe that both represent in their literature is so consistently and insistently masculine and homosocial.

Much has been made of Cleaver's vicious and repeated attacks on women and gay men. In almost every treatment of this issue, however, Cleaver's misogyny and homophobia have been chalked up to male privilege and antiquated notions of what constitutes properly black gender and sexual relations. To date, no one has examined seriously Cleaver's tragicomic struggle to construct a black heterosexuality, to finally rid the black consciousness of the dual specters of effeminacy and interracial homoeroticism. One might argue, in fact, that Cleaver's woman hating and fag bashing were, for all his bravado, failed attempts to assert himself and the black community as "straight."

Soul on Ice is in large part an explication of the difficulties of black identity formation within the highly homosocial, homosexual prison. Women, though present, operate only as the means by which social relations between men are communicated. Early in the text Cleaver confesses to having been a racially motivated rapist, perfecting his craft on the bodies of black women before he "crossed the tracks" to seek out his "white prey."[3] Clearly, the abuse of the black female body acts as a means to an end, a type of cultural production in which Cleaver's manhood, his sense of self-worth, is established and articulated. I would be wrong, though, to suggest that Cleaver's ultimate goal is to possess and abuse white female bodies. Women act here only as conduits by which social relations, relations that take place exclusively between men, are represented. Cleaver may indeed be fucking black and white women, but it is white men whom he intends to hurt.

Rape was an insurrectionary act. It delighted me that I was defying and trampling upon the white man's law, upon his system of values, and that I was defiling his women—and this point, I believe, was the most satisfying

*to me because I was very resentful over the historical fact of how the white
man has used the black woman. I felt I was getting revenge. (Cleaver, 26)*

The peculiarity of Cleaver's twisted logic rests not so much in
the fact that he saw sexual violence as an insurrectionary tool.
On the contrary, the rape of women is used regularly to terror-
ize and subdue one's "enemies." The difficulty in Cleaver's logic
rests in the fact that he raped both white *and* black women. Was
he, I must wonder, seeking revenge on the white man when he
violated poor, black female residents of his quintessentially
black ghettos?

This question is not simply rhetorical. Cleaver himself argues
that there is a tendency within some segments of the black
community to understand the black woman as having collaborated, particularly through the vehicle of sex, with the white
master. Thus, raping the black woman could be interpreted as
an attack on the white man's stooge. The black woman becomes
the means of telegraphing a message of rage and resistance to
the white male oppressor, a figure Cleaver recodifies as the Omnipotent Administrator.

It becomes clear that the ultimate target of Cleaver's sexual attacks is always the white man. Both white and black women act
as pawns in an erotic conversation between Cleaver and his white
male counterparts. This fact is emblematically represented in an
exchange between Cleaver and a white prison guard who enters
Cleaver's cell, rips a picture of a voluptuous white woman from
the wall, tears it to bits, and then leaves the pieces floating in the
toilet for Cleaver to find upon his return. The guard later tells
Cleaver that he will allow him to keep pictures of black women,
but not whites.

The clue to how deeply homoerotic the exchange between Cleaver and the guard actually is lies in Cleaver's description of his initial reaction. He writes, "I was genuinely beside myself with anger: almost every cell, excepting those of the homosexuals, had a pin-up girl on the wall and the guards didn't bother them" (Cleaver, 21). Cleaver's pin-up girl acts as not only a sign of interracial desire but also a marker of his heterosexuality. This fact, which seems easy enough to understand, actually represents a deep contradiction within Cleaver's demonstration of the black male heterosexual self. It points directly to the disjunction between the reality of the interracial homoerotic, *homosexual* environment, the prison, in which Cleaver actually lived and wrote and the fantasy of black heterosexuality that he constructs in his narrative.

Indeed, Cleaver's one rather ethereal representation of heterosexual love seems artificial and contrived, coming as it does from the pen of an admitted serial rapist and committed homophobe. He spends some time in *Soul on Ice* describing the exchange of "love" letters between his lawyer, Beverly Axelrod, and himself. Strangely enough, there is little of Cleaver, the rapist, in these works. His love seemingly transcends the corporeal. By turns he describes Axelrod as a rebel and a revolutionary, a person of great intelligence, compassion, and humanity, a valiant defender of "civil rights demonstrators, sit-iners, and the Free Speech students." And just at the moment when he has produced her as bodiless, transcendent saint, he interjects,

I suppose that I should be honest, and before going any further, admit that my lawyer is a woman . . . a very excellent, unusual, and beautiful woman. I know that she believes that I do not really love her and that I am confus-

ing a combination of lust and gratitude for love. Lust and gratitude I feel abundantly, but I also love this woman. (Cleaver, 32–33)

I am less concerned with pointing out the obvious homoerotic reference than with voicing how strikingly measured and cerebral his relationship with Beverly Axelrod actually was. Lust and gratitude are distinct from "love," which is presumably a type of transcendent, *trans*sexual appreciation for the intrinsic worth of the individual.

Yet Cleaver's description of his noncorporeal, nonfunky love for Beverly Axelrod can only redouble upon itself. It directly challenges the claim that Cleaver's work is a product of the stark reality he has experienced. Cleaver has, much like the white man, the Omnipotent Administrator he so despises, excised his own penis, his lust, his physical self from the conversation.

The Omnipotent Administrator, having repudiated and abdicated his body, his masculine component which he has projected onto the men beneath him, cannot present his woman, the Ultrafeminine, with an image of masculinity capable of penetrating into the psychic depths where the treasure of her orgasm is buried. (Cleaver, 175)

Still, even as Cleaver decries the bodilessness of the Omnipotent Administrator, his love for Beverly Axelrod is no more physical than is the white man's for the ultrafeminine. Beverly Axelrod is unlike the victims of Cleaver's rapes in that she is all intellect and no body. The "sexual" passion between the two is even more rarefied than that of the Omnipotent Administrator and the Ultrafeminine because there is never even the promise of physical contact, raw sex, but only endless *literary* representations of their desire. Beverly Axelrod should be understood as a fiction, or rather as the site of yet another fictional exchange. In this manner, the idea of heterosexual normality becomes a caricature of itself. The body gives way to intellect, lust to love.

"Love" was for Cleaver always the terrain of conceptual struggle. Indeed, "love" becomes in *Soul on Ice* the very site at which normality is constructed in contradistinction to the sense of boundary crisis that mitigates against the production of a stable black masculinity. Perhaps the most telling moment, in this regard, is Cleaver's confrontation with his white intellectual mentor, Chris Lovdjieff, a prison teacher and a man whom Cleaver describes as "The Christ." Lovdjieff introduces Cleaver to what the great novelists and playwrights had said of love. He reads poetry on the subject and plays his students tapes of Ashley Montagu, then instructs them to write responsive essays. Cleaver writes that he cannot love whites, quoting Malcolm X as evidence:

How can I love the man who raped my mother, killed my father, enslaved my ancestors, dropped atomic bombs on Japan, killed off the Indians and keeps me cooped up in the slums? I'd rather be tied up in a sack and tossed into the Harlem River first. (Quoted in Cleaver 47)

Lovdjieff responds in a fit of tears to what he takes to be a personal attack. Cleaver remarks, "Jesus wept," then leaves. Soon thereafter, the San Quentin officials begin to curtail Lovdjieff's access to the prisoners, finally barring him from entry altogether.

The ideological work that the reenactment of this oedipal ritual accomplishes is both to detach Cleaver and his narrative from the deeply homoerotic relationship he maintains with Lovdjieff and to clear the way for a purely black masculinity. It is important to remember here that the country was in the midst of rather striking changes in the manner in which the official "reality" of both race and sexuality were articulated. In 1949, the United Nations Economic and Social Council (UNESCO) launched a study to identify means by which racism might be eradicated. The result of these efforts was a document, written by the same Ashley Montagu whose words Lovdjieff attempted to use as a bridge between his young protégé and himself.

Montagu, who began life as Israel Ehrenberg in London's East End, was trained as an anthropologist first at the University of London's University College and eventually at Columbia where he received his graduate education under no less a light than Franz Boas.[4] By the time he wrote UNESCO's statement on race, he already had published widely in the field, developing a critical apparatus that not only called for a markedly relativistic understanding of "racial attributes" but that altogether called into question the efficacy of maintaining race as an analytical category.

For all practical social purposes, "race is not so much a biological phenomenon as a social myth. . . . Biological differences between ethnic groups should be disregarded from the standpoint of social acceptance and social action. The unity of mankind is the main thing." (Quoted in Shipman, 163)

I suggest again that when Cleaver severs his ties with Lovdjieff, he is helping to reestablish an ontological economy that takes racial difference as primary. The resolution of the crisis represented by their relationship leads to the renormalization of received racial thinking.

At the same time, it is important to point out that the post–World War II period witnessed an incredible bifurcation in the means by which sexual desire was articulated and actualized. The typical narratives of the postwar sexual ethos would have it that Americans rushed into a sort of suffocating domesticity, erecting, in the process, an image of the nuclear family that would maintain a stranglehold on the nation's consciousness for at least two decades. There was also, however, a huge increase in the visibility of homosexual communities, particularly in the nation's cities, the same locations that were opening themselves more and more to black immigrants.[5] The most prominent chroniclers of the black urban male experience, including not only Cleaver, Baldwin and Thomas but Claude Brown, Malcolm X, and Amiri Baraka all reference the increased visibility of the urban homosexual. For these authors, the black homosexual represented the very sign of deep crisis of community and identity that confounded the boundaries of black normality.

II

Piri Thomas's narrative *Down These Mean Streets* proceeds in much the same manner as Cleaver's. Like his Anglo contemporary, Thomas gains his sense of manhood from within the confines of racist urban America. Like Cleaver, and indeed like a variety of late-twentieth-century black male "autobiographers," most notably Malcolm X, his loss of freedom opens the path by which he *gains* his "freedom." Thomas uses the experience of prison to resurrect that part of himself that presumably has been squelched by the realities of racism and poverty, affecting in the process a *counter*scripting of the antebellum slave narratives. It is as if the literal loss of control over the self returns the narrators to the primal scene of black subjectification, the moment when the black, particularly the black man, enmeshed within a system defined by the policing of black bodies, turns for "escape" to the life of the mind, much as Douglass turns to literature and literacy in his struggle to construct himself as "free."

Thus, the focus becomes the immense effort necessary to maintain one's humanity or one's subjectivity, in the face of intense pressures to suppress or deny them. Unlike the antebellum slave narratives, however, in which the black male slave risks being brutalized viciously or, worse yet, having his familial and conjugal prerogatives trampled upon by licentious white men, the twentieth-century black male narrators are in danger of being *homosexualized*. I have discussed this phenomenon in the work of Cleaver already. I add here that Thomas's understanding of himself is altogether mediated by his relationships with men. His adoration for his father gives way to his loyalty to the gang and then finally to his respect for the prison ethos. Throughout, the homosexual acts as the emblem of the border between the inside and the out. Thomas deploys the figure of the homosexual at precisely those moments when the complex ambiguity of his "standing" within his various communities is most apparent, those moments when he cannot avoid a declaration of his status as either The Insider or The Out.

The great difficulty of maintaining the distinction between the homosexual and the homosocial is made explicit from almost the beginning of Thomas's narrative. The young man begins to develop as an adult, as a subject constructed by—but nevertheless greater than—the various identities he inhabits, at precisely that moment when he proves that he has heart, *corazon*, and is accepted into an all-male Puerto Rican gang. The test of his spirit, the challenge that he must accept if he is to be integrated fully into the gang's social life, is a fist fight, a strikingly physical struggle of wills between Thomas and the gang's leader, Waneko.

He had corazon. *He came on me.* Let him draw first blood, *I thought,* it's his block. *Smish, my nose began to bleed. His boys cheered, his heart cheered, his turf cheered.* "Waste this chump," somebody shouted.

Okay, baby, now it's my turn. He swung. I grabbed innocently, and forehead smashed into his nose. His eyes crossed. His fingernails went for my eye and landed in my mouth—crunch, I bit hard. I punched him in the mouth as he pulled away from me, and he slammed his foot into my chest.[6]

By standing his own in this fight, Thomas not only gains acceptance into the gang but initiates a relationship with Waneko that lasts over many years. This fact is not so terribly remarkable. The idea that violence often helps to strengthen the bonds between men is hardly new or surprising. Still, I argue that the strikingly physical nature of the contest between Thomas and Waneko ought to alert us to the multiple levels on which this interchange resonates. Thomas allows Waneko to draw first blood out of deference to his position in the neighborhood and the gang. The abuse that the two young men mete out to each other in the course of their fight should not be understood, then, simply as a sign of masculine aggression. Thomas is not allowed into the gang solely because he is good with his fists. Instead, the emphasis is on that elusive entity, heart, that place of deep feeling and masculine determination to which the young Puerto Ricans gain access through ritualized violence. The fight between Thomas and Waneko is at once an act of aggression *and* an act of love.

I am supported in this claim by the fact that the gang members expend so much energy denying homoerotic feeling, even while all of them, including Thomas, seek out and willingly engage in (homo)sex. It is telling that only a few pages after the fight scene the young men decide to stretch themselves to the limits of their masculinity by visiting the apartment of a trio of stereotypically effeminate gay men. Indeed, their interaction with the three homosexuals is itself designed to reflect their own hypermasculinity. They assure themselves, "Motherfuckers, who's a punk? Nobody, man," as they "jumped off the stoop and, grinning, shuffled towards the faggots' building" (Thomas, 55).

The episode in the gay's men's apartment is from the very outset overdetermined by the intense ambiguity that suffuses the extremely homosocial world of the gangs. The faggots, the *maricones*, stand in for the constant danger that the macho young men, with their relentless emphasis on masculinity and the male body, will stumble themselves, inadvertently or not so inadvertently, across the line that separates the homosexual from the homosocial.

I had heard that some of them fags had bigger joints than the guy that was screwing. Oh shit, I ain't gonna screw no motherfuckin' fag. Agh—I'm not gonna get shit all over my peter, not for all the fuckin' coins in the world. *(Thomas, 55)*

The fag refuses, in this passage, to conform to the boys' stereotypes. His joint, his penis, the marker of his worth within the logic of patriarchy, is larger than that of the guy doing the screwing, the real man who stands in for Thomas and his comrades. Even more striking is the fact that Thomas's fear, the fear that he will screw a fag (thereby compromising his own masculinity), the fear against which he must reassure himself constantly, turns upon the idea that he will get shit all over his penis. This aversion to feces points directly to the immense ambiguity, the boundary crisis, that the homosexual represents. Instead of Thomas's pulling blood from the gay body, much as he regularly pulls blood from the bodies of his fellow gang members and presumably also

115

from the bodies of recently deflowered (female) virgins, he takes only shit from the fag, shit that acts as evidence of the nonproductive, perverse nature of the homosexual act.

What I am interested in here is not the cataloging of homosexual content in the work of late-twentieth-century black male autobiographers but instead a reading of homosexuality that pays attention to the way in which the homosexual stands in for the fear of crisis and chaos, or, rather, the fear of slipping to the outside, that pervades the work of both nineteenth- and twentieth-century black writers. As the young "heterosexual" Puerto Rican men enter the apartment of the young "homosexual" Puerto Rican men, as the former fuck the latter and the latter suck the former, it becomes difficult, even in the face of the "straight" men's many protestations, to maintain a distinction between the two. It becomes nearly impossible to continue the inside/out binarism.

The rather lengthy group sex scene that Thomas describes takes on a strikingly surreal aspect. The air that they breathe is heavy with the smell of marijuana smoke, thereby pushing *all* the young men beyond their *normal* limits, creating the space of the gay men's apartment as a type of liminal terrain; we might even say a *no*-man's land. Moreover, the effect is not simply that the *normality* of their erotic lives is jettisoned but also that the sexual act becomes transposed onto a variety of experiences and sites.

I opened my eye a little. I saw a hand, and between its fingers was a stick of pot. I didn't look up at the face. I just plucked the stick from the fingers. I heard the feminine voice saying, "You gonna like thees pot. Eet's good stuff."

I felt its size. It was a king-sized bomber. I put it to my lips and began to hiss my reserve away. It was going, going, going. I was gonna get a gone high. I inhaled. I held my nose, stopped up my mouth. I was gonna get a gone high . . . a gone high . . . a gone high . . . and then the stick was gone, burnt to a little bit of a roach. (Thomas, 58)

Though this passage is taken from a scene that is heavily determined by the notion of profligate sex and sexuality, there is apparently no sexual activity at all. No penis, vagina, breasts, or buttocks are here to alert the reader that what we are experiencing is a type of *sexual* intercourse. There is neither blood nor feces to act as evidence of the all-important penetration. Indeed, the very fact that this passage lacks the normal markers of sexual activity is what produces it as a representation of profligacy. Here the erotic content is transferred from the sexual organs to the lips, a key site of homoerotic, homosexual pleasure. As the pot stick enters Thomas's lips, chipping away at his reserve until he is altogether gone, or, we might say, spent, sexuality is severed from its association with the genitals and thus with heterosexual reproduction.

For his part, Thomas accepts neither the passive nor active role. Though he receives the stick of pot into his mouth, he does the penetration himself, plucking the stick from between extended fingers, fingers attached to a never visible face. Still, it is once again the size of the faggot's pot stick, or, rather, his joint, that intrigues the youth. He is literally blown away by the innate power of this king-sized bomber, reaching, in the process, a type of homoeroticized epiphany.

Then it comes—the tight feeling, like a rubber band being squeezed around your forehead. You feel your Adam's apple doing an up-an'-down act—gulp, gulp, gulp—and you feel great—great, dammit! So fine, so smooth. You like this feeling of being air-light, with your head tight. (Thomas, 59)

Perhaps the most telling aspect of this rather remarkable scene in Thomas's narrative is the fact that when he returns from what I will call his drug-induced orgasmic moment, he immediately sets about tidying up the mess that he has just described. I do not mean to suggest, however, that he denies the homosexual activity. On the contrary, the descriptions of the various acts taking place between men are rather straightforwardly rendered.

I tried to make me get up and move away from those squeezing fingers, but no good; . . . I pushed away at the fingers, but it grew independently. If I didn't like the scene, my pee-pee did. . . .

I dug the lie before me. Antonia was blowin' Waneko and Indio at the same time. Alfredo was screwing La Vieja. The springs on the bed were squeaking like a million mice. . . . Indio's face was white and scared and expectant, but his body was moving in time with Antonia's outrage. I tightened my own body. It was doing the same as Indio's. It was too late. I sucked my belly and felt the hot wetness of heat. I looked down in time to see my pee-pee disappear into Concha's mouth. I felt the roughness of his tongue as it both scared and pleased me. I like broads, I like muchachas, I like girls, I chanted inside me. . . . Then I heard slurping sounds and it was all over. . . .

I smelled the odor of shit and heard Alfredo say, "Ya dirty maricon, *ya shitted all over me."*

"I'm sor-ree," said La Vieja, "I no could help eet."

"ya stink'n faggot—." . . . I heard the last sounds of Alfredo's anger beating out against La Vieja—blap, blap, blap—and the faggot's wail, "Ay-eeeeee, no heet me, no heet—" (Thomas, 61)

We can see, in this passage, the reestablishment of the line separating the inside from the out at precisely the moment at which the spectacle of homosexual intercourse is realized most fully. Thomas maintains a distinction between himself and his sexual desire, producing, for a moment, the former as the victim of the latter. It is his "pee-pee" that refuses to allow him to exit this scene. Moreover, the word "pee-pee," with its connotations of childhood innocence, helps exonerate Thomas from any responsibility for the act in which he is engaged. Instead, by reasserting his genitalia as the privileged site of sexual pleasure, Thomas rescues himself from the never-never land of oral and anal eroticism. It is Concha, a name that can be translated as either shell or pussy, who steps to the nether side of the phallic economy, allowing his mouth to be "used" like the presumably (dis)empowered site of the vagina. Throughout, Thomas reminds himself that what he is experiencing is a lie. The satisfaction he feels is the product of a simple substitution, the mouth for the vagina, in which his pee-pee is fooled but he is not. He chants, "I like broads, I like *muchachas*, I like girls," as if to remind himself, in three different vernaculars, that the spectacle of his pee-pee within the faggot's mouth is but a representation of, or perhaps, a signification upon the truth. And if this were not enough, the scene ends with the smell of marijuana smoke giving way to the stench of shit, the proof that the boys have stumbled beyond the limits of normality, sullied themselves in the confusing, if always false, pleasures of the outside. As Alfredo beats La Vieja, the old woman, a man who despite his name is described as no more than thirty, the sexual and erotic economies seemingly have come back into order, the highly stylized—and stereotypical—rendering of La Vieja's screams: "Ayeeeeee, no heet me, no heet—" acting as irrefutable evidence of the incommensurability of *el macho* with *la maricon*.

It is striking that even as Thomas paints the faggot as the quintessential outsider, he seems incapable of dispensing with him. Homosexuals and homosexuality intervene throughout the text to help Thomas give definition to his fledgling masculinity. It is during their attempt to rob a gay nightclub, or rather a site in which there are nothing but "faggots and soft asses," that leads to Thomas's arrest and incarceration. The would-be robbers—Thomas, his friend, Louie, and their two white accomplices, Danny and Billy—are thwarted in their efforts because they underestimate the ability of the homosexual to turn their expectations and desires back in on themselves. When Billy jumps to the stage and interrupts the drag show taking place, the audience refuses to respond in a fit of hysteria as he had expected. Instead, they laugh, taking him for one of the performers. It is as if the sight of a poor, undereducated man attempting to assert his masculinity, his lack of lack, is itself a greater spectacle than the transvestite performance. It is only after he fires two shots over their heads, shattering the mirrors in the process, that they give him their full attention, or rather reflect back the image that he wants to see. Of course, the entire affair is bungled. Thomas is shot by an undercover police officer whose own incognito status within the gay bar implicates him as fully in the transvestite spectacle as any of the drag performers. The whole scene turns, in fact, upon the recognition that things are not always what they seem. The "women" on stage are not really women. Thomas is not really a macho gangster, but instead just a Puerto Rican teenager who when struck by the bullet of an undercover police officer reverts to an infantile state: "I felt like a little baby, almost like I was waiting to get my diapers changed" (Thomas, 237). "Mommie . . . I don't . . . Mommie, *no quiero morir* . . ." (Thomas, 238).

I have argued already that the prison acts as a primary site for the articulation of a late-twentieth-century Black American masculinity. When the black narrator enters prison, he returns to the primal horde, as it were, a state in which the brothers are corralled together by the capricious violence and deprivation enacted by the father. Here the oedipal crisis has not been enacted but only imagined. Thomas's focus remains on the unattainable female, his former girlfriend, Trina, even though the truth of his situation is that homosociality has given way altogether to homosexuality.

the real action was between men. If you weren't careful, if you didn't stand up for yourself and say, "Hands off, motherfucker," you became a piece of ass. And if you got by this hassle, there always was the temptation of wanting to cop some ass. (Thomas, 262)

In prison the rational norms no longer continue to operate. In spite of all his *corazon* and macho bravado, even Thomas is tempted to "cop some ass."

We should be careful not to slip into the trap of conceptualizing the situation that Thomas describes as simply the opposite of normality.[7] The danger that Thomas confronts when he gives voice to his own nascent homosexual desire is not simply that he will implicate himself further as an outsider. On the contrary, the episode in the apartment of the three effeminate gay men had proven already that he could maintain his macho image even in the midst of homosexual intercourse. The danger is that he will lose hold on the logic of the inside/out binarism altogether, that he might forget that his desire for his girlfriend, Trina, is real, while his "desire" for men is only a substitution.

One time. That's all I have to do it. Just one time and it's gone time. I'll be screwing faggots as fast as I can get them. I'm not gonna get institutionalized. I don't want to lose my hatred of this damn place. Once you lose the hatred, then the can's got you. You can do all the time in the world and it doesn't bug you. You go outside and make it; you return to prison and you make it there, too. No sweat, no pain. No. Outside is real; inside is a lie. Outside is one kind of life, inside is another. And you make them the same if you lose your hate of prison. (Thomas, 263)

Thomas clearly sees the danger of blurring the distinction between the inside and the out. He is afraid to screw faggots, not because it is displeasing but because it will allow for the articulation—and actualization—of an alternate logic of pleasure. Prison becomes, in this schema, not simply the wretched underside of normal life, but an alternative site of meaning, truth, even love and life.

This is represented emblematically by two characters whom I will treat briefly here. The first, Claude, is a black man who is extremely attracted to Thomas and who offers his reluctant paramour a host of prison treasures if he will agree to be "his daddy-o." Thomas refuses. Claude then takes up with another prisoner, Big Jules, a man sentenced to a life sentence for cutting someone up into little pieces. The couple celebrate their union in a wedding complete with preacher, best man, and attendants.

The second is Ruben, a muscular and exceptionally violent inmate, who is attracted to Thomas's "cousin," Tico. The naive youth accepts Ruben's many presents upon his arrival in prison until he receives a note from the older man, expressing his real intentions.

Dear Tico:
Since the first moment I saw you, I knew you were for me. I fell in love with your young red lips and the hair to match it. I would like to keep on doing things for you and to take care of you and not let anybody mess with you. I promise not to let no one know about you being my old lady and you don't have to worry none, because I won't hurt you none at all. I know you might

think it's gonna be bad, but it's not at all. I could meet you in the back part of the tier cell hall and nobody's going to know what's happening. I've been doing a lot for you and I never felt like this about no girl. If you let me cop you, I'll do it real easy to you. I'll use some hair oil and it will go in easy. You better not let me down 'cause I got it bad for you, I'd hate to mess you all up.

Love and Kisses

XXX

You know who

R.

P.S. Tear this up and flush it down the shit bowl. (Thomas, 266)

The most intriguing thing about Claude's desire for Thomas and especially Ruben's desire for Tico, particularly as it is represented within his note, is the fact that in both instances the emphasis is precisely *not* on sex but instead on the production of a new type of (homosexual) romantic relationship. Claude wants not only an intercourse partner but a husband, a daddy-o, one willing to express his commitment within a "public" ceremony. Moreover, one might argue that, instead of pining away for some unattainable outside, some reality beyond his grasp, Claude empowers himself through the structures of the prison itself, subverting, in the process, the many constraints on his freedom. He refuses to understand Big Jules as solely a sadistic murderer but instead reconfigures him as husband, lover, mate. Ruben, for his part, never even attempts to sever his tendency for violence from his love. He assures Tico that he will just as quickly "mess him up" as love him. Yet the highly romantic nature of his note is undeniable. Strikingly, his love for Tico begins not at the cock or anus but at the lips and hair, the redness of which excite his passion. The beauty of the young man's red mouth and lips belies the necessity of the woman's (red) vagina. Ruben assures Tico, "I never felt like this for no girl" and then closes with a series of salutations that seem jarringly feminine and trite: Love and Kisses, XXX, You Know Who, R. He reminds Tico, in a postscript, to flush his note down the *shit* bowl, emphasizing once again the *counter*-rationality of his desire.

III

I turn to the work of James Baldwin, who achieves in his *Giovanni's Room* an incredibly well developed explication of the manner in which normative modes of masculinity produce and are produced by a certain species of (aberrant) racialized homosexuality. The progress of Baldwin's early career might be narrated, in fact, as a series of successively more explicit and stark representations of the black abject, or, as I demonstrate later, the ghost of the black homosexual. The whisper of adolescent longing for distant fathers and virile young men in *Go Tell It on the Mountain* gives way in *Another Country* to the tragically inverted "straight" man, Rufus, who, on the one hand, passionately fucks his white girlfriend, a woman Cleaver refers to as a southern Jezebel, and, on the other, takes a white male southern lover, or, again to quote Cleaver, "lets a white bisexual homosexual fuck him in the ass."

To be fucked in the ass by the white man is not simply to be overcome by white culture, white intellect, white notions of superiority. Nor can it be understood solely as the undeniable evidence of the desire to be white. Instead, Cleaver's fear is that Baldwin opens up space for the reconstruction of the black imaginary such that the most sacrosanct of black "truths" might be transgressed. The image of the white (male) southerner fucking the (unwilling) black woman resonates with a long history of Black American literature and lore in which the licentious white man acts as the absolute spoiler of black desire. The image of the white (Southerner) fucking the black *man*, however, throws all this into confusion.

On the one hand, we see a rescripting of Frederick Douglass's famous account of the whipping of his aunt Hester. The black male subject is no longer able to remain, in the closet, as it were; instead he takes the woman's place on the joist, becoming himself the victim of the white man's scourge. On the other, it seems that the white man needs not force his "victim" at all. The reader cannot find comfort in the idea that the image of white male "abuse" of the black male body is but a deeper revelation of white barbarism. The black subject willingly gives himself, becoming in the process the mirror image of the culpable female slave whom Angela Davis has described so ably. One might argue, in fact, that the spectacle of interracial homosexual desire puts such pressure on the ideological structures of the black national literary tradition that it renders the continuation of the inside/out binarism nearly impossible.

These are the issues that shape the narrative of Baldwin's second novel, *Giovanni's Room.* This work, which is widely thought of as Baldwin's anomaly, the work with no black characters, the work in which Baldwin stretches, some might say unsuccessfully, to demonstrate his grasp of the universal, has been neglected by students of both black and gay literature, many of whom assume Baldwin had first to retreat from his blackness in order to explore homosexuality and homophobia. I argue, though, that the question of blackness, precisely because of its very apparent absence, screams out at the turn of every page. As we have seen already, the *non*existence of the black, particularly the black homosexual, is a theme that Baldwin starts to develop as early as *Go Tell It on the Mountain*. My reading of *Giovanni's Room* proceeds, then, via an exploration of the absences in the text. I suggest that Baldwin's explication of Giovanni's ghost-like nonpresence, his nonsubjectivity, parallels the absence of the black from Western notions of rationality and humanity while at the same time it points to the possibility of escape from this same black-exclusive system of logic.

Baldwin initiates his discussion of race in the very first paragraph, alerting the reader that even though there are no blacks present, this is yet a race novel:

I watch my reflection in the darkening gleam of the window pane. My reflection is tall, perhaps rather like an arrow, my blond hair gleams. My face is like a face you have seen many times. My ancestors conquered a continent, pushing across death-laden plains, until they came to an ocean which faced away from Europe into a darker past.[8]

There are a number of clues in this passage to alert the reader to the ideological work accomplished within Baldwin's text. His use of the autobiographical "I" both conflates his identity with that of his protagonist, David, and signals us that what he is interested in here is the subject of identity formation. David's consideration of his reflection demonstrates, moreover, Baldwin's fascination with the relationship of the Object to the Inverse, the One to the Other. David is indeed the *real life* (American) character who considers the fate of the already, or the almost already dead Giovanni. In the process, he faces away from Europe, away from whiteness, and from received notions of masculinity and sexuality to a nebulous darker past.

Like Cleaver, then, Baldwin, in *Giovanni's Room* faces the task of examining the relation of the black to the white, the body to the mind. It is the desire for the other's body, in the person of Giovanni, that dictates the action of this text. Giovanni's nominally white, southern Italian body is bought and sold in the course of the novel. Giovanni becomes simply a creature of his body, a creature of sex and desire, by which other men are able to gauge their own humanity. That is to say, the paradox of the *male* homosexual is precisely that he usurps the woman's position as the site on which, or by which, fictional relationships between subjects are represented.

This explains why the central tragedy of the novel is the fact that Giovanni is never able to achieve his one true dream, the transcendence of the ideology of the corporeal: "Me, I want to escape . . . this dirty world, this dirty body. I never wish to make love again with anything more than the body" (Baldwin, 35). It is not that Giovanni simply despises his flesh. On the contrary, he loves his flesh. It is the *idea* of his flesh, or rather, the fiction that his flesh represents, that he so despises. He wishes to make love again, but only with his body, a body onto which others will no longer project notions of either filth and bestiality or respectability and autonomy. It is telling that Giovanni begins his process of pushing against the strictures of Western thought not in Paris but in Italy, where he leaves behind his wife after their failed attempt to produce a child, the marker of both husband and wife's authenticity within the patriarchal economy. Giovanni struggles throughout not only to escape the position of the other but to produce a new identity, to move beyond the logic of self and other altogether. His work in Guillaume's bar, his relationship with David, and especially his squalid, overcrowded, and never quite finished room are all testimony to his desire to achieve an alternative "realness," to enter the world of the living without becoming trapped there, to create a universe of his own making.

It is at this juncture that Baldwin's work so profoundly intersects both Cleaver's and Thomas's. Like his heterosexually focused, heterosexist counterparts, Baldwin is concerned with both the body and the image of the body constructed by the white (European) mind. More important, all three men, even as they are divided by the yawning chasm of sexual desire and practice, give voice to the fear that the fiction of a pure heterosexuality no longer can be maintained, that the processes by which the "black" male subject is imagined as autonomous, virile, and invulnerable can no longer be rendered transparent. In each case, it is the homosexual who stands in for this concern, the homosexual who becomes the (scape)goat. It is almost as if the dissolution, in the gay body, of the strictures concerning "proper" black male sexual desire and practice parallels the dissolution of a transparent Black American national consciousness. The homosexual is there when the "respectable" black male protagonist gives way to the criminal Eldridge Cleaver. He stands by as Anglo-American centered notions of race and "blackness" are thrown into disarray by the Spanish-inflected "English" of the New York–born Puerto Rican Piri Thomas. Indeed, it is the search for the homosexual that drives the narrative of *Giovanni's Room*, a novel in which Baldwin, an author who has at times represented the apex of (Black) American liberal sentiment, abandons Black America, as it were, producing a text in which received racial thinking is inverted, if not *sub*verted.

The character Giovanni might be read, in fact, as a rather odd and startling twist in Cleaver's notion of the Supermasculine Menial, the black and immensely physical opposite of his Omnipotent Administrator. The white bourgeoisie, the French Guillaume and the Belgian (American) Jacques, are competing constantly to claim both Giovanni's labor power and his sex, a process that necessarily restricts Giovanni to the realm of the corporeal and the dirty and that creates him at once as both the brutalized black male slave *and* the sexualized black female slave. In this sense, Giovanni has been dirtied, much as Puerto Rican boys are sullied with shit as they cross the line between the inside and the out in their traffic with already marginal—and ambiguous—homosexuals. As Baldwin suggests, *the* central task of modern life is the struggle to rid oneself of the dirt:

what distinguished the men was that they seemed incapable of age; they smelled of soap, which seemed indeed to be their preservative against the dangers and exigencies of any more intimate odor. . . . (Baldwin, 118)

Strikingly, cleanliness acts as the very definition of manhood in this passage. The men are *cleanly* delineated from women, *cleanly* established as members of a community, *cleanly* recognized as insiders and subjects.

The struggle for cleanliness, the denial of the body that might protect one from the dangers of intimate odor, is precisely the struggle that David faces when he looks into his darker past. He attempts throughout to maintain a *clean* masculinity, to maintain his sense of respectability even as he, much like Thomas's gang, is pulled ever more deeply into the dirty muck. David's immersion into the Parisian *demimonde* has as much to do, then, with his desire to understand himself as *not* dirty, as *not* vulnerable, and, indeed, as *not* homosexual as with any real affinity for the people by whom he finds himself surrounded.

Most of the people I knew in Paris were, as Parisians sometimes put it, of le
milieu *and while this milieu was certainly anxious enough to claim me, I
was intent on proving, to them and to myself, that I was not of their company. I did this by being in their company a great deal and manifesting toward all of them a tolerance which placed me, I believed, above suspicion.
(Baldwin, 32–33)*

This precisely replicates the process of denial that I demonstrated
in my discussion of *Soul on Ice* and *Down These Mean Streets*. Real
identity, meaning heterosexual identity, is formed through concurrent acts of repression and projection. The homosexual non-
subjects of *le milieu* not only reflect David's own subjectivity, creating him as a real man; they also stand in for the erasure of
boundaries that render the entire real/not real logic unworkable.

David's abandonment of Giovanni for his female lover, Hella,
a woman whom we hear about only in the second person until
rather late in the novel, is both a demonstration of his heterosexuality *and* his authenticity. With Giovanni, David can exist only
in the shadowy and confined spaces of back alley cafes, late-night
bars, and, most especially, Giovanni's cramped, suffocating, and
disheveled room. It is this room, much like the gay men's apartment in Thomas's narrative, that acts as the marker of Giovanni's
gallant, if quixotic, effort to construct a space for himself.

*But it was not the room's disorder which was frightening; it was the fact
that when one began searching for the key to this disorder, one realized that
it was not to be found in any of the usual places. For this was not a matter
of habit or circumstance or temperament; it was a matter of punishment or
grief. (Baldwin, 115)*

I think it important here that we not get stuck in a reading of this
passage that would proceed solely from the assumption that the

homosexual Giovanni has been punished for his efforts to break out of normality by being banished to the realm of "the never quite finished," "the always in process." That is not to say that I intend to disallow this reading altogether. Instead I would suggest also that the joy that David and Giovanni are able to achieve, however briefly, is itself a product of this same disorder. "In the beginning our life together held a joy and amazement which was newborn every day" (Baldwin, 99). The attraction for both David and Giovanni is that they are obliged to recreate themselves—and the room—daily. Each has refused already to settle down. Both have left their "fatherlands." Both throw off the strictures of male heterosexuality. Both leave behind the mores and values of *le milieu*. Perhaps, then, the greatest tragedy—and the promise—of this work is that, while David and Giovanni are cast out of the "mainstream," neither is able—or willing—to inhabit the margin. They are not the other, but the vehicles of the abject.

It becomes impossible for either to claim status in the "real" world or even its underside. Giovanni cannot simply give in to the abuse and manipulation of Guillaume. Instead, he kills him, creating himself as the marginal's marginal, the fugitive. Like both Cleaver and Thomas, he is eventually caught and incarcerated, remaining in prison until he undergoes the ultimate dissolution of the inside/out binarism, death. David has run away already from "America," which in this instance refers not simply to a geographical location or a complex of political and social structures but also to a patriarchal economy that produces maleness as the lack of lack, a fiction that David is never able to maintain. After the death of his mother, the family fiction is thrown into a profound crisis. His domineering aunt becomes the primary source of power and order in the household, re-embodying his father, in the process, such that the notion of masculine invulnerability is exploded. Indeed, the tragedy that David brings with him from America is precisely that he both sees and knows his father. "Fathers ought to avoid utter nakedness before their sons. I did not want to know—not, anyway, from his mouth—that his flesh was as unregenerate as my own" (Baldwin, 26).

David can never go home to the wide open plains of America. And yet, even as David attempts to create his (American) female lover, Hella, as a surrogate for his homeland, as he mounts one last desperate attempt to save himself, to create for himself an identity that can be seen and acknowledged within respectable (American) society, he is always haunted by the dual specters of Giovanni and his own homosexuality. David becomes himself a type of ghost, growing ever distant from Hella, retreating into a world of memory and denial to which she has no access.

And I look at my body, which is under sentence of death. It is lean, hard, and cold, the incarnation of a mystery. And I do not know what moves in this body, what this body is searching. It is trapped in my mirror as it is trapped in time and it hurries toward revelation. (Baldwin, 223)

Here again we see the reference to death, the site at which the distinctions between the inside and the out, the self and the other, give way, allowing only the articulation of ghost-like subjectivities. Strikingly, David's ghost body becomes inexplicable. He can no longer fashion a narrative by which to describe it. It is distinct from the self, which remains a victim to a type of body logic that he cannot yet understand.

It is at this point that we can see most clearly the process by which the figure of the homosexual is conflated with the figure of the ghost, a process that occurs throughout the production of

Black American literature. The specter of the nonproductive, unauthentic, weak, effeminate, and antisocial homosexual had not, it seems, been exorcised with the virulently homophobic diatribes of Eldridge Cleaver, nor even with the deaths of Rufus and Giovanni. In the process of creating the authentic black subject, a process that necessarily involves concurrent practices of negation and projection, one has always to resurrect the ghost of the black devil. That is to say, we must point to that which is unauthentic, base, and perverse in order to adequately define the borders of black "realness." At the same time, as we travel through the underworld, the muck, the shit that is represented by the black homosexual, we are able to access, if only briefly, new modes of understanding and existence that seem to wait just beyond our grasp. Thus, the black homosexual continues as such a potent figure in American literature because he represents not only a site of death, but also and importantly, of resurrection. As David says of Giovanni, "in fleeing from his body, I confirmed and perpetuated his body's power over me. Now, as though I had been branded his body was burned into my mind, into my dreams" (Baldwin, 191).

I opened this essay with two epigrams: "Thou shalt not seethe a kid in his mother's milk," and "*Chivo que rompe tambor con su pellejo paga,*" or the goat who breaks the drum pays with his hide. Both statements, taken from different if not altogether dissimilar religious "texts," the Bible and the proverbs of the Cuban Abakua societies, reflect a profound concern with the question of perversity. To cook the goat in the same milk with which it has been nourished is to subvert a number of "self-evident" truths, among them the distinctions between right and wrong, inside and out, such that it becomes impossible to maintain the coherency of the society's logical order. At the same time the very existence of the prohibition bespeaks the reality of a desire that stands outside received logic. Indeed, it may be perverse to eat the kid prepared with its mother's milk, but this does not make it less enjoyable.

That the concern with boundary crisis, with the goat's tendency to break out of its proscribed roles within society should be repeated among Cuban Yoruba-based religious groups reflects not only the intersection of Christianity with New World religions but also the fact that the articulation of the perverse and the grotesque is absolutely necessary to the production of a variety of national cultures. As Coco Fusco has suggested, even while the Abakua proverb points directly to the grave consequences of troublemaking, it demonstrates the necessity of the untamed "outsider" to the continued creativity of the rest of the community.[9] As James Baldwin's Giovanni is slaughtered and as Thomas's effeminate gay men are fucked and beaten, a type of music is produced, a music that points the way to new modes of existence, new ways of understanding, that allow the community to escape, however briefly, the systems of logic that have proven so enervating to the black subject. The importance of the (scape)goat, then, is not so much that with its death peace returns to the village or that crisis ends. The point is not simply to expurgate all that is ambiguous and contradictory. On the contrary, as the kid is consumed and the drum is beaten, the community learns to gain pleasure from "the possibilities just beyond its grasp." It receives proof of its own authenticity and insider status while leaving open a space for change, perhaps even the possibility of new forms of joy. The boundaries are for a moment reestablished, but all are certain, even hopeful, that once again they will be erased.

VI The Shock of Gary Fisher

nigger, youre dead with your zipper open and your dick hanging
   out
youre dead with a booger hanging out your nose and your zipper
   open and your dick hanging out
youre a dead nigger hanging with your dick out and a big booger
   and snot hanging out your nose
nigger, yous dead with your guts and your dick hanging out your
   nose
so, yous dead, nigger, with your dick cut off and hanging out your
   mouth
so, yous dead with someone elses dick *in* your mouth
so, yous *alive* with someone elses dick in your mouth, nigger

                    —GARY FISHER, "Being Dead"

The shock of Gary Fisher, and his collection *Gary in Your Pocket*,
the ugly, unsettling, if strangely erotic effect of poetry and prose
written by an already dead writer who never accessed print in his
lifetime, is the uncanny directness of it all, Fisher's perverse rationality. One is left speechless by his unassailable common
sense. The nigger is absent even and especially when his body is
present. Dick, booger, snot, and guts notwithstanding, the nigger
is inevitably and irrevocably dead. The enumeration of the body's
attributes, the articulation of nigger corporeality, is taken, in and
of itself, as evidence of death, established as the vocabulary of a

black postmortem. Fisher repeats, then, one of the most regularly articulated paradoxes of western modernity: the nigger is not alive but nonetheless strangely, inexplicably available for animation. Thomas Jefferson writes:

[The blacks] are more ardent after their female: but love seems with them to be more an eager desire, than a tender delicate mixture of sentiment and sensation. Their griefs are transient. Those numberless afflictions, which render it doubtful whether heaven has given life to us in mercy or in wrath, are less felt, and sooner forgotten with them. In general, their existence appears to participate more of sensation than reflection. To this must be ascribed their disposition to sleep when abstracted from their diversions, and unemployed in labour. An animal whose body is at rest, and who does not reflect, must be disposed to sleep of course.[1]

For Jefferson the black is always physically available but nonetheless never emotionally, mentally, or spiritually there. More important, this paradox, the notion of a physically present but socially dead black, has infected all arenas of American cultural and intellectual life. Thus, I argue that even the philosophical and aesthetic ambitions of what has come to be known as Black American culture turn precisely on the necessity of establishing a live blackness, a corporeality that does something other than announce social death.[2] To put the matter in the most base terms, life begins for the black at precisely the moment when she takes control of her own black body, wrestles her subjectivity from the hands of white masters in much the way that Frederick Douglass (within the pages of his narrative) wrestles his freedom from the hands of the slave breaker Covey.[3]

But for Fisher this model of the slave in conflict with the master, a model that directly references the master/slave dyad within

Hegel's *Phenomenology*, cannot be understood as simply noble or, perhaps better put, antiseptic. Instead, Fisher forces us to look more deeply into the irony of this struggle. Indeed, he brings clarity to one of the points that I attempted to stress in the preceding chapter. Even as we express the most positive articulations of black and gay identity, we are nonetheless referencing the ugly historical and ideological realities out of which those identities have been formed. Fisher thus insists that within the process of creating (black) identity one necessarily traffics in the *re*articulation of the very assumptions embedded within Jefferson and Hegel. There is no black subjectivity in the absence of the white master, no articulation in the absence of degradation, no way of saying "black" without hearing "nigger" as its echo. The import of reading Fisher, then, is that by frankly bringing this reality into public discourse he gives us the opportunity to imagine new ways of articulating self and other, black and white. Fisher writes of one of his many sexual encounters with white dominant men:

Didn't I want to die a hundred times this way? Wouldn't I be happier? I hadn't seen his cock, didn't know it would be so big, so unmanageable—hadn't I always wanted to die this way? He pushed toward my throat, curled me still tighter, and drove my head down on it, still talking about death like it was our only alternative. Maybe I understood this mechanism, I'd become the middle of, understood its strength, its unrelenting, its selfishness and selflessness. I tasted his salt, his ooze, and my throat jumped, but I could not dislodge him. (Fisher, 65)

The idea that Fisher can articulate even a half-hearted desire to die while giving himself to his master is, in and of itself, a rather remarkable feat within the various traditions of American and Black American literature. What I believe to be more striking still is that Fisher provides a perfect rearticulation of the master-slave dynamic that I have been at pains to demonstrate. The slave is literally kept from speaking so that the master might maintain his fantasy of dominance, his fantasy of having created the nigger in his own image. Fisher's partner continues, "Its okay if you choke Arab," demonstrating that Fisher's silence allows the master to produce a world in his own image, a world in which a Black American might be turned into an Arab in the course of a single good face fucking.

I do not want to stray too far, however, from what I believe to be the more subtle, more perverse, more radical aspects of Fisher's aesthetic. As Fisher works to demonstrate the debauchery of his master(s), he never allows the assumption that he is himself an innocent. Indeed, the very fact that Fisher's published words are those that define the exchange between master and slave, black and white, demonstrates agency, articulation, that is not squelched by the masters's cock. More important, Fisher is eager to demonstrate that his articulateness is not simply an act of resistance to the master's dominance but also an effect of that dominance. "My throat jumped, but I could not dislodge him" is a phrase that suggests both that the master's cock stops the Negro's expression *and* that it is a vehicle of that expression. In this sense, master and slave can no longer be understood as separate subject positions, but instead must be seen as complimentary components in a process of expression.

I haven't read Hegel yet. Why haven't I read Hegel when I'm somewhat in love with this? I'm afraid to know. Half of this is the wandering, the obscurity, the possibility of surprise (and yet the other half is a fixed equation, inevitable—when I get there I'll be able to say I've always known this would happen to me—but I'll come to that admission as through a dream, still half unbelieving). (Fisher, 185)

Gary Fisher dares to know. He confronts—*without* reading Hegel—that which is embedded within Hegel, the fixed equation, the knowledge of both master and slave subjectivity, a knowledge so blunt, so bruising, that it literally can kill. Images of often deluded and always abusive whites abound in *Gary In Your Pocket*. But this is old hat for Fisher and, I believe, most of his readers. What is more stunning, what shocks is that Fisher says, without flinching, that the black is not inculpable, that she is as much perpetrator as victim. As we will see, Fisher's constant return to the erotics of slavery and his insistence that the black is always an active and potent agent within these erotics not only places him among the most perverse of Black American authors but suggests a model of black subjectivity and black expression that at once masters and deforms some of the most cherished idioms of Black American vernacular tradition.

The question that this leaves us with is, "How can we read Gary Fisher as a black man?" Given my argument that Fisher repeatedly takes up the particularly shocking notion of a Negro racial identity not only produced in direct relation to white hostility but produced in a manner that takes sublime pleasure in the white's domination, it taxes the imagination to place him neatly alongside Toni Morrison, John Edgar Wideman, James Baldwin, or even the growing number of self-identified black gay writers.

Saturday, November 2, 1985
So I want to be a slave, a sex slave and a slave beneath another man's (a white man or a big man, preferably a big white man) power. Someone more

aware of the game (and the reality of it) than myself. I want to relinquish responsibility and at the same time give up all power. I want to, in effect, give in to a system that wants to (has to) oppress me. This made Roy (Southern, white, 40 + man) attractive to me—not wholly this. This made Tony so attractive to me. If T.K. had been the least bit dominating (encouraging) I don't know where I'd be now. (Fisher, 187)

It is important that we remember how rare this direct (re)articulation of a subjectivity "repressed within itself" is within traditions of Black American writing. Indeed, one might have to travel as far as the much maligned Phillis Wheatley to find another author who even comes close to expressing a desire for enslavement, much less an understanding of a (black) articulateness that is dependent upon the interposition of the masters. Like Wheatley, Fisher refuses the easy distinction between master and slave, insisting instead that there is no possibility for the expression of a (liberated) black identity in the absence of white masters. Indeed Fisher's contribution to the race-inflected philosophical and aesthetic traditions with which we are concerned is to insist upon recognition of the intimate connections between both those practices that exclude the black, kill him, as it were, and those that would resurrect him.

"Can you get your hand in there? Three fingers?"

He was pushing my hand, bending my wrist this funny way, telling me to bunch up my fingers—three, no, four—into a tube, "loosen yourself up for my cock." I told him it wasn't possible, that I didn't get fucked anyway, but he kept pushing my own hand into me, making the grunts of enjoyment that perhaps he thought I should be making. Reminding me that I belonged to him—exclusively to him—even more than I belonged to myself, and that I would enjoy this whether I wanted to or not. (Fisher, 63)

Again, black subjectivity is figured as a function of white degradation. Twisted wrist, fingers forced uncomfortably into resisting ass suggest an awkward, unnatural body put to the service of an equally unnatural white master. And yet we also see the fiction of white dominance put on display. The cues of a submissive, repressed subjectivity—those grunts, the reminder of ownership and forced enjoyment—all emanate from the purported master himself, while the slave remains infinitely aware of the intricacies of the transaction.

I am not attempting to rehabilitate Fisher for those wary of perverse black subjectivity. On the contrary, Fisher's genius turns on his ability to spoil all our expectations, to deform our most cherished models of human subjectivity. Even in his resistance, Fisher produced nothing like the independent, manly blackness that we see displayed in figures like Douglass. The gesture that Fisher illustrates—the black man with three, possibly four, fingers up his ass, the black man caught in an act of self-pleasuring (or self-degradation depending on one's point of view), the black man taking direction from the obviously self-deluded white—is hardly designed to rearticulate our most precious models of black subjectivity. Instead, Fisher offers an almost withering critique while also maintaining obvious contact with the idioms of Black American exceptionalism, the many ways in which we imagine ourselves as an essentially innocent people.

In Fisher's formulation, the black is finally whole. The self-pleasuring, self-degrading black gay brings to mind the figure of the Sankofa, the Akan icon that, much like the phoenix, commands us, "Go back and get it!," the very icon that has been taken up by black filmmakers in both the United States and Britain, that indeed has become the emblem of New York's African burial ground, a powerful symbol itself of the continuity and antiquity of a certain Africanized nobility. And yet there is a difference. Fisher reminds us that retrieval, including historical retrieval, always involves the very white "master" whom the "retrieval" is presumably designed to reject.

Friday, November 9, 1984

It felt good sitting on Roy's cock. It felt good being folded in two and deeply fucked by the man. Jamie too with so much rhythm it was all I could do to hold on for him—he was a wonderful fucker. . . . I only have one big regret—that I won't suck a million more, that I won't suck that special one (whoever it belongs to) a million times; that I won't be folded up and made one with a stud. (Fisher, 185)

"Folded up and made one with a stud" is the phrase that most intrigues me in this passage. Its resonance with the emblem of the Sankofa is immediately apparent. Fisher is folded back in upon himself, allowed to see the continuity of the struggle between master and slave. Again Fisher forces the notion that the black is made whole, made one, only in the presence of the (white) stud, the master. At the risk of being overly repetitive, I will say that what distinguishes Gary Fisher's work, what I have called the shock of Gary Fisher, is the manner in which it insists upon the *necessity* of the (abusive) white, the master, in all projects of black self-definition.

Here is where I disagree somewhat with the introduction to Fisher's collection by Don Bolton. Entitled "Gary at the Table," the essay places Fisher squarely within a tradition of black gay cultural production exemplified by the work of Marlon Riggs and Melvin Dixon. And, indeed, when one arranges *Gary in Your Pocket* alongside Marlon Riggs's *Black Is/Black Ain't*, it is immediately apparent that both men were eager to integrate the fact of their own sexuality, their own history, and their own impending death within their respective projects. Moreover, the startling fact that neither was able to complete his work in life but instead relied upon the assistance of editors to bring their projects to fruition deserves much more attention than I can grant it here. Still, I argue that, where Riggs's work actively challenges simplistic notions of black identity, it nonetheless continues the assumption of a black seamlessness whereby the black dead come to intercede—and actively so—in the lives, the living experience, of the animated black. I am reminded here of those sequences in *Black Is/Black Ain't* in which Marlon, naked and alone in the forest, follows a path that he tells us has been prepared by Harriet Tubman. We are led to believe that his own death is not an end but simply a transmogrification of sorts, a return to the past, Sankofa in flesh.

This is not simply a performative gesture, one's own hand being forced up one's own ass as proof of someone else's dominance, someone else's subjectivity. I suggest, in fact, that to produce a too easy relationship between Gary Fisher and his "brothers," men whom he only infrequently hails in the course of his writing, absolutely belies the radical—or, perhaps better put—perverse thrust of his writing. Is this black gay male literature? Yes, if the quality of one's literature is simply a factor of phenotype and the reports of one's sexual practice. If, however, we mean to ask whether Fisher participates fully in the established idioms of Black (gay) American literary and cultural production, then I must express at least some doubt.

I think, in fact, that a better mode of inquiry when examining Fisher's work would be to consider just how thorough he was in his absolute refusal of (Black American) normative narratives of human subjectivity. The electricity of the multiple—and sometimes violent—encounters that he has with white dominant men is turned on not simply by pain or racial insults but also and importantly by his inability to distinguish his own desire to *de*create from the white's desire to dominate. When he is called "nigger" by a lover, he is never sure how exactly to register the effect. Thus, he rejects the assumption that that which is performative is necessarily innocent, necessarily outside the realm of reality, beyond ethical and political consideration. We are not asked to read his work from the vantage point of a well-established cultural relativism. The pain he endures, the semen he ingests, the degradation he faces do have results. Fantasy can kill. "And then, didn't some people become addicted to their own poisons and begin to reason that the disease was the cure, or that their personal cure was hidden somewhere within the topiary of their personal addiction?" (Fisher, 42)

For Fisher the individual who would know is never innocent, never wholly separate from even the most ugly truths that she uncovers. In order to master fully the intricacies of Western modernity, one must expose oneself to degradation and disease, even though the likely consequence of such exposure is death. My thinking in this matter has been strongly influenced by the fact that Fisher believed he contracted H.I.V. as a student at the University of North Carolina during one of his many study sessions in the Wilson Library, that his mastery of his subjects was coterminous with the disease's mastery of his flesh.

I've amazed myself today by getting just about all my homework done, and atop this I'm understanding it. Calculus was a little puzzling, but I'm get-

ting the hang of it. I whizzed right through some limits. I made short order of my German and English reading by making today a library day. I may as well make good use of my excuse for going to Wilson library every night. I know it's really for the off chance of meeting a guy who'll have sex with me (hopefully the *guy). Still, I feel good about getting so much work done. I'll continue to frequent the library because it's as conducive to work as it seems to be for homosexual connections. (Fisher, 139)*

The piling on of forms of mastery—literary, scientific, sexual—is so very overdetermined as to seem obscene. The disturbing notion that in coming to know one comes to die, that wisdom is toxic, is an idea that Fisher continued to rework throughout his writing career. In his last days of life he comments that he takes the painful, discomfiting treatments meted out by his doctor in much the same way that he had taken treatments from his lovers, his teachers. He suggests that his situation is not at all particular, not hemmed in by blackness, gayness, precociousness. Instead, as he attempts to establish a solidity under the sign of Gary Fisher, as he forces fingers up his ass, always with the assistance of an outsider, a nominally proficient master, he comes to create an image of subjectivity that is available to us precisely because it is fractured, uneasy, always in a process of reformulation, precisely because it mirrors the obscene nature of all subjectivity.

Tuesday, May 22, 1979
Hope you've enjoyed it this far, fellow reader. Half of it's in tribute to you! (Fisher, 133)

I think it would be helpful here to invoke Hortense Spillers's useful, if somewhat difficult, distinction between body and flesh. The flesh, "that zero degree of social conceptualization that does not escape concealment under the brush of discourse," precedes the body. Moreover, it is the flesh that has been most insulted in the long nightmare of American racialism, the flesh that contin-ues to quiver under the shock of the master's whip.[4] Following Spillers, one might easily conclude that mastery is, in fact, never possible in the absence of the flesh's immolation. As Fisher sug-gests repeatedly, abused flesh is the very sign of a well-established black subjectivity.

The better lie—what do I tell Helmut tomorrow? What do I tell him tonight when I leave a message on the office machine, or when I dare to call him at home? How do I make quick amends for skipping work today? What story do I act out? who do I pretend to be when I step into that office tomorrow morning?

The plan—the visual device—might involve a bruised lip, a red eye, a scratch on my forehead (all of which, right now, are real—real products of a furious face-fucking I took last night and this morning from a leather-clad gentleman . . .) and perhaps a two-inch square shaved patch of scalp which I'll cover with a spotty white bandage (this, an elaborate, I know, and per-haps unnecessary attention-getter/reality-enhancer, as well as a bit of self-immolation/punishment for the acts that got me into this situation in the first place). (Fisher, 83)

Fisher is again stunningly direct. His production of a normative (black) self is absolutely dependent upon signs of his flesh's degra-dation. He is real, believable, only insofar as he is able to access the abused flesh of his forefathers, to demonstrate a suffering that literally strikes at bone. Face-fucking becomes, therefore, the em-blem of the relation of mastery to flesh that I have suggested. Fisher's own speech is stopped as he receives instruction from the master, instruction that must hurt in order to be effective. At the same time, the master's abuse of Fisher's flesh (bruised lip, red eye, scratched forehead) allows for the (re)production of the real Negro, the abused Negro, the Negro who is alive. "So yous *alive* with someone elses dick in your mouth, nigger."

Fisher's work leaves one with the distinct understanding that the white master is necessary to the project of black historical recovery precisely because his abuse of flesh (mimicked by Fisher through his "abuse" of language) is what truly connects the black modern to her enslaved ancestors. Certainly, if it is true that what connects generations of Black Americans and other persons of African descent is the fact of some sort of shared biology and the "white" reaction to the same, then it becomes clear that each strike against a black body completes the cycle, returns us to our roots, provides a bridge to a less than noble past.

Christmas Eve, 1985
I UNDERSTAND this self-slaughter, but it scares me. I'm trying to decreate. Trying to go back; not to an easier time, but a more honest one. Shit, slave, nigger, cocksucker; like the wind and the darkness, the Auroras of Autumn. I'm doing it with sex and society, bludgeoning myself with misconceptuous facts, or the fictive facts that were "in fact" bludgeons then. No, I'm doing it with words. . . . *(Fisher, 188–189)*

The equivocation in this passage is particularly telling. Fisher seems to not understand what actually produces his "decreation," his (sexual) actions, or the language that he uses to make sense of those actions. He finally settles on words as the vehicle of his own self-destruction cum self-revelation, but here I think Fisher misses how fully challenging his aesthetic actually is. He has consistently refused the easy mind/body distinction on which so much in modern Western thought and social practice has been established. He has insisted not that fucking is somehow secondary to thinking, but, on the contrary, that the two are interrelated and perhaps indistinguishable acts. Thus, Gary Fisher's expression is activated by his white master, the leather-clad gentleman who delivers a furious face-fucking. In this way, it becomes impossible to use the phrase "black expression" without recognizing some necessarily physical, sexual, erotic component embedded within it much in the way that we recognize similar components in the child's *expression* of milk from its mother's breast. Fisher's master becomes then not simply the abuser, the enemy, but the nurturer and provider.

12/11/90 Wednesday (by an hour and a few seconds)
Sperm is perfect nigger food and piss perfect nigger drink and a committed nigger should be able to live, to thrive off this nourishment alone. Piss and sperm nourish the nigger body and feed his black soul. Sperm feeds the wish, the already thwarted potential for the nigger to seek more than a life as a urinal and sperm bank. It feeds the wish but only leads to more wishes, greedier, hungry wishes that only sperm can fulfill. . . . Sperm is more important than the nigger body itself and will ultimately consume him. He must feel toward this purpose, this reward to the exclusion of all else. . . . The nigger takes his hot sacrament from the cocks of men who know where a nigger should be, why he should be, how he should be, and find pleasure in reaffirming that I AM PROUD TO BE A NIGGER. (Fisher, 239)

The shock of Gary Fisher turns squarely on his fierce articulation of what lies just beneath the surface of polite, "civil" American race talk. The life of the nigger is so caught up in the debauchery of the white master that even when "nigger" is translated to "black" it is still possible to sense the faintest hint of the raw milk smell of cum on the breath.

I have written these comments as a way to make sense of the curious phenomena of Gary Fisher and *Gary in Your Pocket*. In particular, I have been struck by how difficult the text seems to have been for those people—white, black, and otherwise—who have encountered it. Indeed responses have ranged from righteous indignation toward the text and its editor, Eve Sedgwick, to a rather maddening inarticulateness, a sort of collective shrug at a document that demonstrates some of the ugly intricacies of what is often saddled with the euphemistic label "queer." In this instance, however, I have tried neither to defend Fisher nor to suggest anything noble in Fisher's having died before ever publishing a word of his remarkable prose. What I *have* been concerned with, however, is the difficulty that Fisher creates for those of us he left behind. Fisher neither establishes the fairy tale black, white, red, yellow, brown beloved community so feebly articulated by innumerable rainbow flags; nor does he signal a separate, resistant black (gay) identity. What Fisher tells us is much more difficult, more shocking than any of this. Fisher goes beyond demonstrating that black/white intimacy is necessary and inevitable. Instead, he insists that if we are to maintain the clear distinction between the black and the white, this intimacy will never move beyond the ugly display of the master's dominance over the slave and the ugly scene of the slave's yielding to the same. There is no way to say "black" without hearing "nigger" as its echo. Fisher allows none of us to remain innocent. That is his challenge and his promise.

MAN

VII Living as a Lesbian

In 1985 Barbara Smith came like a fresh wind to Chapel Hill. She brought with her a vision of home unlike anything I had imagined. Home held out promises of redemption and nurturance, acceptance and love. Home was populated with brothers and sisters so unlike my own "natural" family in their politics, their progressiveness, their passion. At home we would recreate ourselves and our world, fashion a new mode of being, map a way for living in which the vision of the black freedom struggle would be realized in the daily interaction of black lesbians and gays. In coming home, I told myself, I would finally be able to articulate that which I had known all along, the centrality of the black woman, the black faggot, the so-called black underclass, and especially the black lesbian to the project of redeeming America. Armed with strong doses of Audre Lorde, Pat Parker, Cheryl Clarke, and Donna Kate Rushin, I felt, for a brief moment in my life, as if I knew in which direction to place my feet, saw clearly the road before us.

The most general statement of our politics at the present time would be that we are actively committed to struggling against racial, sexual, heterosexual, and class oppression, and see as our particular task the development of integrated analysis and practice based upon the fact that the major systems of oppression are interlocking.[1]

My sister had been in early life the quintessential daddy's girl. To him she was "his heart," the proof of his own self-worth, his princess to be protected from boys, men, and the great unfriendly world. It seemed to all of us that only a moment had passed before her long hair, fancy dresses, and sassy little-girl style gave way to cigarettes, a Jheri curl, unquestioned prowess on the basketball court, and then eventually to her first woman lover, Rose. News of the passionate love affair between seventeen-year-old bulldaggers hit my family like the news of death or war. After months of histrionics and therapy, my parents packed first my sister and then me off to live with our aunt in Brooklyn for a boring summer of softball and Coney Island. When we returned, our parents announced their divorce, or, rather, our mother announced that she would be leaving our father.

My sister's lesbianism had by all indications been cured. She started a tempestuous relationship with Darryl, another impressive basketball player and the father of her child. She suffered through years of drug and alcohol abuse and raised her son, in working poverty, always stuck in the shadow of my parents' smugly secure comfortableness and my own unquenchable thirst for success. She pushed forward, however unfruitfully, into the mystique of heterosexual acceptability until unexpectedly Rose, her ex-high school lover, suddenly reappeared, moved in, and began receiving well-chosen gifts from my parents during the holidays.

> *Afraid, jealous, or stuck in some foaming*
> *funk I learned from her in the circumstances*
> *of her loneliness, I push away from my lover.*
> *This hotness, this coldness still*
> *in her aging she tricks me.[2]*

My students and I have been discussing Audre Lorde's *Zami* in a monstrously large Harlem building with few windows. We keep the door to the classroom open to save ourselves from roasting inside the six-inch-thick cement walls. I present the text to them like a scarce and delicious morsel. They snatch it up, hungrily consuming what they like, leaving the rest to scavengers.

"I'm not a lesbian, still I can relate."

"I'm Caribbean and these Caribbean writers just get under my skin."

"Was she abused as a child?"

"Was she afraid of black people?"

"I didn't read the whole book, but. . . ."

Audre Lorde, Audre: Poet, Mother, Sister, Lesbian, Warrior, Cancer Survivor, was for them—and for me—just the third assignment in a fourteen-week syllabus, sandwiched in between a collection of Lower East Side writers and Alfred Kazin's *Walker in the City*. They liked her, they said. I talked about her being the poet laureate of New York, one of the great prophets of multiculturalism and the concept of overlapping identities. They blinked back at me and argued among themselves about whether lesbians could walk the streets of Harlem holding hands.

To whom do I owe the power behind my voice, what strength I have become, yeasting up like sudden blood from under the bruised skin's blister?[3]

"He looks just like a girl," well-meaning ladies would giggle as they passed by me, sitting on the front steps, my Afro braided down into neat cornrows. Other children would respond cruelly that indeed I was a boy, that it was only my fat body and long hair that so obfuscated my sex. And yet even they could not resist taking me around by the hand on Halloween nights, when dressed in a skirt and stockings, I would present myself as a rather delectable treat on neighbors' doorsteps.

"Stop acting like a sissy," my father would bark at me, his eyes fixated on my limp wrist as I crossed the street from the school bus.

"Mira Loca!" my Dominican neighbors would yell years later as I issued forth, in full butch queen regalia, from my newly rented Washington Heights apartment.

I have acquired this ill-fitting masculinity at considerable cost. There were years during my adolescence when men would start to scream at me as I walked out of public restrooms, assuming that I was some crazy or radical woman breaking into their most sacred domain. In graduate school I became the first male T.A. for the "Introduction to Women's Studies" lecture. My sections filled up with the few men taking the course. One of them would eventually break down in class as he recounted the details of his having been sexually abused. Another wrote to me privately that I was the only thing standing in the way of his acting on unspecified rape fantasies. I assigned him the grade check, as opposed to check minus or check plus, and told him that this was one of the most interesting things he had written.

This anger so visceral I could shit it
and still be constipated.
My ass is sore with the politics
of understanding the best given the circumstances.
I could spit this anger
and still choke on the phlegm.[4]

My lesbianism takes me to dyke parties in Brooklyn, small clubs hidden away among the West Side warehouses, the odd women's gathering, and a wealth of impromptu therapy sessions. I know all the young black female film and video makers: Cheryl, Shari, Dawn, Vejan, Yvonne, and even Michelle, not to mention Jackie W., the children's writer; Pamela, the performance artist; Cathy, the Ivy league professor and AIDS activist; bald Jackie B., the erotic poet; Jewelle who needs no introduction; and, of course, Barbara, the mother of us all. I am asked with a regularity that never ceases to surprise me for my sperm and then asked, ever so gingerly, to step quietly aside.

My files are packed with back copies of *Sinister Wisdom, Off Our Backs, On Our Backs,* and *Conditions.* I have recently removed my copy of J. R. Roberts's bibliography, *Black Lesbians,* from my bookcase, afraid that this most precious piece of lesbian ephemera might be damaged on my crowded shelves. I continue to keep my three issues of *Stallion, Male Pictorial,* and *Honcho,* my two issues of *Drummer* and *Mandate,* my four issues of *Advocate Men,* and my single issues of *Inches* and *Torso* in a box under my bed.

The book you are holding in your hands is a kind of miracle. The fact that hundreds of Black lesbians have found the courage to commit their lives and words to paper is miraculous.[5]

To become myself I have become a lesbian, or at least that's what I have been told. I have found my way into dozens of women's beds, been thoroughly schooled in the intricacies of women's relationships, learned to sit quietly and listen as the many vulgarities of "The Man" are rehearsed:

> *how like a man*
> *is the ku klux klan*
> *it comes in the night*
> *to wag its ugly shaft*
> *to laugh at the final climax of its rape*
> *as rope chokes out the final cry of "why?"*
> *blood blurring sight of a naked cross.*[6]

And yet. And still. Even as I stand before the bathroom mirror, my dick tucked between my legs so that only the bushy triangle of pubic hair is showing, I continue to smell my own heavy man's smell, a scent not very different from the musky sweetness my father left behind in my childhood memories. Of late I have taken to rubbing my face along the cocks and balls and inside the buttocks of my lovers, hoping that in their scent I might find something of my own, or my father's, or his own unknown father's. I lick the sweat off bellies spilling over too-tight jeans, suck gobs of chest hair, and underarm hair, and scrotum hair into my mouth, gorging on the rough texture, begging to be pinned down to the bed, to be penetrated by a vigorous and vibrant masculinity. My lovers whisper, "Whose pussy is this?" as they struggle to slip their cocks into my ass. I haven't the heart to answer simply that it is my own.

> *Adrift on this windless sea*
> *this independence*

we have brushed and skirted
shells
compelled by current.[7]

In 1985 Barbara Smith came like a fresh wind to Chapel Hill. She brought with her a vision of home unlike anything I had imagined. It would be years before I would look up to find that as I searched for home I continued in my isolation. It was the death of Pat Parker that first alerted me to the fragility of both our dreams and our community. First her then Joe Beam then Donald Woods then David Frechette then Rory Buchanan then James Baldwin and Roy Gonsalves then Audre Lorde herself. In response I wrote:

I could have fucked him
Head on rumpled pillow
Ass lifted towards heaven
Like she cat
In season
In heat

I might have cut into flesh
Leeched out blood
Bitten into gristle
And Swallowed

>   *And yet*
>   *And Still*

I tried saving him long distance
Tied up phone lines preaching brotherhood
Wrote treatises on community
Debated love and metaphysics at the institute

Took clever men to bed

Shall I scratch his name onto parchment
Press it to my lips
Arrange it among the relics on my altar?

Shall I build a memorial
Great Edifice Reaching forth to God
Higher than misery?

I showed this, my only attempt at poetry as an adult, to my boyfriend at the time, who told me that the "She Cat" line made him uncomfortable. We broke up. I left for the comfort of my girlfriends. He started dating women. We both resisted the somewhat Afrocentric, Brooklyn-centered black lesbian and gay community, finding that our own deepest desires had turned back in on themselves.

I'm a queer lesbian.
Please don't go down on me yet.
I do not prefer cunnilingus.
(There's room for me in the movement.)[8]

Cheryl phones on an early weekday morning looking for $100 and advice. I write a check for fifty and remain on the telephone for hours debating the relative merits of worry versus denial. She complains that too many of the wrong kind of women love her. I answer that that's my problem exactly. We laugh, make plans to see each other, and hang up. The two of us maintain a type of charming delicacy with each other. I respect her boyishness as she cherishes my effeminacy. We are a couple, mentioned in one breath as dinner parties are planned, given to public quarrels over the minutiae of everyday life, constantly aware of each other's steps and jealous of the intrusion of outsiders. Our lesbianism runs deep. We are drawn together because of our profound love of women, our unquenchable thirst for companionship, our hot blooded sexual passion, and our constant struggle to find and create home. She chides me to help her write her story. I respond by looking hard at her small breasts, pulling from her the details of her menstruation and resisting the urge to cover my penis, floating in the bath water, as she passes by the tub.

> Sweet words and warm this time—
> not like the last time salty and frigid
> over some money I owed her [9]

Living as a lesbian continues for me to be a process in which I am constantly brought back, in my search for spiritual perfection, for transcendence, to my body, to the luscious beauty of my heavy thighs and hairy chest, my fleshy ass and strong hands. And still I continue to love and desire "her" body, Cheryl's body, Yevette's body, Joanna's, Daphne's, Pat's, Sabhia's, and Nicki's bodies, not simply the image or the promise, but the texture of their hair, the color of their skin, the smell of their sweat.

In 1985 Barbara Smith came like a fresh wind into Chapel Hill. She brought with her a vision of home unlike anything I ever had imagined. It was then that I began the process of becoming a lesbian. It is only recently that I began to understand lesbianism as a state of being that few of us ever achieve. To become lesbian one has to first be committed to the process of constantly becoming, of creatively refashioning one's humanity as a matter of course.

Coda

By becoming lesbian then I have done nothing more nor less than become myself.

I had expected to end this piece with these words, forcing all of us, myself included, to reevaluate what it means to be labeled lesbian, gay, straight, bi, transgendered, asexual. And yet this is not enough. For, even as I recognize the difficulty of giving definition and meaning to our various identities, I also realize that as I struggle to lay claim to my lesbianism I am always confronted with the reality of my own masculinity, this strange and complex identity that I continue to have difficulty recognizing as privilege.

It was a Friday afternoon in September when I had my first bathhouse experience. I'm not sure what I expected, or wanted. In truth, I was compelled more than anything else by Samuel Delany's description in *The Motion of Light in Water* of his visit to the Saint Marks Baths in the early sixties. I thought that it would be exciting, that perhaps within this outlaws' territory I could throw off the stifling fears and anxieties that shape and constrain our lives, sexual and otherwise. I even felt that, given the name of the enterprise I was about to visit, "baths," there had to be something intrinsically cleansing and healing about them.

Now I find myself asking whether in the bathhouse, the most sacred of male enclaves, where my masculine body and affected macho style increase my worth in the sexual economy, I am still lesbian. Is it lesbianism that spills out of the end of my cock as bald-headed men with grizzled beards and homemade tattoos slap my buttocks and laugh triumphantly? Is it lesbianism that allows me to walk these difficult streets alone, afraid only that I will *not* be seen, accosted, "forced" into sexual adventure?

All my bravado, my will to adventure is caught up, strangely enough, with the great confidence I have gained from "The Lesbian." And yet, this confidence, this awareness of my own body, of my own independence, takes me to places where she dares not go. Perhaps then I am not a lesbian at all, but rather like a drag queen: by day a more or less effeminate, woman-loving gay man, by night a pussy, a buck, the despoiler of young men recently arrived from the provinces and the careful tutelage of their loving mothers. What I know for certain is that this self, this lesbian-identified gay man, is in constant flux. I live like a lesbian, *as* a lesbian because I know no better way of life. Still, I live beyond her in a province that continues to be reserved exclusively for men, all the while reaping the many fruits of sexual apartheid.

Me, I want to escape . . . this dirty world, this dirty body. I never wish to make love again with anything more than the body.[10]

Perhaps in my next life I will be done with these questions of identity altogether, will cherish fully the body that I am given, begin to see it neither as burden or weapon but only as the vessel of my existence. Perhaps in my next life I will have given up finally this constant struggle to explain who I am not: not woman, not white, not straight, not you and start to revel in the limitlessness of my boundaries. Perhaps each one of us will recapture that which has been lost, start again to accept and acknowledge the profound ambiguity and uncertainty of this existence. It is then and only then that we will find home.

In 1985 Barbara Smith came like a fresh wind to Chapel Hill.

It's Raining Men

Notes on the Million Man March

Perhaps the most curious feature of the 1995 Million Man March was the way that this massive political demonstration, at least twice the size of the historic 1963 March on Washington, actually worked to reinforce the racial commonsense of the nation. At a moment when the enemies of Black America had consolidated with frightening determination, Minister Louis Farrakhan, his supporters, and even his detractors encouraged the notion that at the root of the difficulties facing Black Americans is a certain male lack—an inability, or unwillingness, to take responsibility as *men* to stand up for community and self.

It was probably an unintended irony that the rhetoric of the march organizers echoed Daniel Patrick Moynihan's infamous 1965 report, "The Negro Family: The Case for National Action," with its diagnosis of pathologies plaguing black families and communities. This resonance, which went largely unremarked, is cen-

tral to the way the march forced so many of us to rehearse the assorted racial, sexual, and political identities by which we define
ourselves and that define us. "Who are you?" the march asked.
"Black or not-black? Man or not-man?"

It should be clear to most observers that the way Farrakhan
and the other march organizers answered these questions—with
appeals to a revitalized patriarchy—worked to reinforce tradi-
tional gender norms. What is less obvious is the way that this
black spectacle restaged the *racial* commonsense of the nation,
the same commonsense that animates much of the conservative
rhetoric about issues and polices most directly associated with
black communities, especially affirmative action and welfare. In
the face of shrinking public resources and an evangelical zeal to
"reinvent" (read: dismantle) government, Black Americans were
once again advised that self-help is the best medicine. The black
man was instructed to return home and start providing for kith
and kin, to stop making excuses about the scarcity of legitimate
well-paying jobs, and to access his inner manhood, that great and
mysterious wellspring of masculinity hidden deep within his psyche, waiting to be harnessed to the project of a beautiful black tomorrow. This all-powerful masculinity was offered as the solution
to, and compensation for, the stark curtailments of resources and
opportunities that confront Black American men (and everyone
else) in this country.

In this light, at a celebration of black masculinity predicated
on the absence of black women, it is interesting to consider the
question of black gay men's participation in the event. For, if the
real message of the march was that it is going to take a heroic
black masculinity to restore order to our various communities, especially poor and working-class communities, then it follows that

black gay men are irrelevant, or even dangerous, to that project. And, if the march itself was intended to re-create a masculine community of agency and responsibility through the archetypical figures of father and son, then the surreptitious presence of the lover threatened to undo the logic of the event itself.

In the weeks prior to the march, the gay press was full of speculation over the proper stance black gay men should take toward Farrakhan, the other march organizers, and the march itself. The National Black Lesbian and Gay Leadership Forum vacillated on the question, finally encouraging gay men to attend and to make their presence known. Activists staged a premarch rally and tried to convince Ben Chavis, the march's executive director, to agree to have an openly gay speaker address the crowd from the podium.

The debate revolved around the question of whether black gay men should support an event so closely identified with Minister Louis Farrakhan, who has made no secret of his homophobia. (In Oakland, California, in 1990 Farrakhan told a crowd, "If God made you for a woman, you can't go with a man . . . you know what the penalty of this is in the Holy Land? Death.") More to the point, black gay men, even if they stayed home, were again confronted with a rather awkward set of questions. Faced with a celebration of a stable—that is, Afrocentric, bourgeois, and heterosexual—black masculinity, gay men who felt compelled by the march had to decide among a number of plausible responses. They could reject the event itself as "not truly black" because of the homophobia and misogyny in which it trafficked. They could think of the march as representative of a flawed blackness that might be repaired by making a significant black gay presence visible at the event (which many did) or by intervening with the march organizers (which a few attempted). And, finally, they could acknowledge the basic logic of Farrakhan's rhetoric. For, if the definition of blackness hinges on heterosexuality, then either blackness and homosexuality are incommensurable (and black gays are not really black) or the notion of blackness is untenable, as witnessed by the undeniable existence of large numbers of black gay men.

This last position, of course, is most difficult to accept. It flies directly in the face of much within contemporary black gay and lesbian thought, which most often represents black gays and lesbians as integral, if beleaguered, members of the black family—witness *Brother to Brother*, *Home Girls*, *Sister Outsider*, works shepherded by Essex Hemphill, Barbara Smith, and Audre Lorde, respectively. Indeed, the gay response to the march dramatizes the fact that there are remarkably few spaces—even those inhabited by black gays and lesbians—in which one might contest the most basic assumptions that underlie American race and gender identity. Even in the midst of raucous and intense disagreement, the idea of race emerges unscathed. Indeed, blackness has been bolstered, insofar as we all were forced, at least those of us who are black *and* otherwise, to scurry for cover under the great black mantle, to fly our colors, the good old red, black, and green, even as we attempted to resist the homophobic assumptions that structured the event.

More than a political demonstration with concrete political demands, Farrakhan's march was a sort of race spectacle. Following Guy Debord, we should look to locate its meaning not in the striking images it produced or in our individual responses but in the social relationships constructed by and through these images. Debord doubts that transcendence can be located within the spectacle. For him, spectacles are never progressive events; rather, they represent and reaffirm the larger society. Debord writes, "For what the spectacle expresses is the total practice of one particular economic and social formation's *agenda*. It is also the historical moment by which we happen to be governed."[1]

His point is well taken. Those of us interested in progressive politics desperately need to reconsider the efficacy of the marches, protests, and demonstrations that convulsed the American public sphere in the past century, as well as the ways in which their themes (civil rights, antiwar, gay pride) are constrained by the nature of the event. Mustering enthusiasm for these events requires a fair dose of ignorance about the contentiousness that invariably surrounds them—disagreements that most often turn on the organizers' unwillingness to push the boundaries of their political and social agendas. I am reminded here of the successful struggle initiated by Anna Arnold Hedgeman to have women included among the speakers on the platform at the 1963 march, as well as the significant opposition to Bayard Rustin's leadership in its planning because of his homosexuality and his ties to leftists. That march has become an important part of the American national memory because it so clearly articulated the rather limited language and values of a liberal America. Indeed, King's "I Have a Dream" speech receives much of its force from the evocation of an ethos that is at once Christian and American nationalist, supporting, in the process, a liberal integrationist agenda that insists upon the expansiveness—and expansion—of the nation.

Mass public spectacles have been a regular means by which changing ideas of race have been disseminated to the American populace. As early as 1895, Booker T. Washington called for black reconciliation with the very whites who were the architects of segregation, disfranchisement, and systematic racist terror, thereby rearticulating the emerging racialist—and segregation-ist—commonsense. Washington's particular genius, evident in his Atlanta Cotton States Exposition speech, was his ability to articulate a conservative racial politics to whites, particularly white southerners, while captivating many blacks with a message that spoke to their basic desire to be admitted as equal participants in American public life. "In all things that are purely social," he argued, "we can be as separate as the fingers, yet one as the hand in all things essential to mutual progress."

It is a compelling irony that the sensibility behind Washington's words should so deeply inform the 1995 rhetoric of Louis Farrakhan. Specifically, both men call for black self-sufficiency, if not self-determination; both swallow, more or less whole, frankly segregationist notions about the proper interaction between the races; and both, oddly enough, subscribe to the myth of America. As Farrakhan proclaimed at the march:

There's no county like this on Earth. And certainly if I lived in another country, I might never have had the opportunity to speak as I speak today. I probably would have been shot outright, and so would my brother Jesse, and so would Maulana Karenga, and so would Dr. Ben Chavis and Reverend Al Sharpton and all the wonderful people that are here. But because this is America, you allow me to speak even though you don't like what I may say.

Of all the curiosities uttered by minister Farrakhan during the march, including the extended numerological analysis, the excoriation of presidents past and present, the religious rhetoric of atonement, and so forth, I was least prepared for this hackneyed bit of American exceptionalism. It was tempting to read this gesture as mere anomaly, the kind of unnecessary bombast that cushions overly long or ambitious speeches. But I suggest we take this piece of Farrakhan's rhetoric seriously—indeed, that we recognize in it the key to his success that day, as he spoke to the assembled masses on the Mall and to the nation.

Minister Farrakhan's particular talent is his ability to sensitize wildly diverse black audiences to their very real oppression while steering them not simply away from a critique of the political and economic structures of the United States but toward a reinvestment in the very ideological processes that work to create and maintain those structures. It is true that Farrakhan regularly points out the evil of the American enterprise: slavery, segregation, disfranchisement, continued and continual racial degradation. But, instead of leading his followers toward radical critique, Farrakhan chooses instead to return again and again to an essentially therapeutic mode in which he plays the role of the good father come back to set the (national) house in order.

At the Million Man March—"a glimpse of heaven," as the Nation of Islam's newspaper, *The Final Call*, had it—Louis Farrakhan put himself forward as the emblem, the ideal type, if you will, of a newly emergent black masculinity. He appeared as a shining exemplar of a renewed Black Man, striking the posture of the stern, if gentle, father, savior, patriarch, messiah. He scorned our enemies while asking us only to look inward, to find the evil therein and to cast it out. If we did so, he prophesied, if only we could learn to humble ourselves, we would surely see a new dawn of cleanliness and order, the Black Millennium. He stood, then, as a sort of Emersonian representative man, embodying a masculinity so pure that simply by gazing upon it one could extinguish the fires of ambiguity and uncertainty that rage in the hearts of black men across America.

The agreement on the part of the march's organizers to dis-
courage black women's participation implicitly shored up Farrakhan's myth making. I never could quite understand why a
demonstration about the plight of Black Americans had to be gendered in the first place. (Wouldn't two Million Black People beat
one Million Black Men?) With this strategy—an obvious insult to
black women—the march organizers showed themselves to be
concerned primarily with lending a certain ontological stability
to men whose identities are increasingly complex. The injunction
to keep the women at home helped channel public debates about
the march into familiar territory, the ongoing "crisis of Black
American gender relations." In that sense, the sexist rhetoric and
the many responses it provoked simply represented business as
usual. It was a forceful restatement à la Moynihan of the terms we
have used to discuss (Black) American cultural, political, and economic life since at least the 1960s.

Fundamental changes in American political and economic life
are currently being debated in a conversation still largely domi-
nated by the Republican right and their Democratic look-alikes.
What is disconcerting about this is the way rhetorics of blackness
(such as Ronald Reagan's "welfare queen" and George Bush's
"Willie Horton") have been coupled not simply with critiques of
black communities but also with even more blistering attacks on
affirmative action, welfare, education, social service initiatives,
and so forth. While the march was still in progress, President
Clinton made a speech at the University of Texas in which, after
distancing himself from Farrakhan, he praised the black men who
attended the event for taking responsibility for themselves and
for *their* communities. He then went on to make a rather predictable speech on race relations in which he suggested, among

other things, that it is not racism that motivates a mother to pull her child close when she passes a black man in a crime-ridden neighborhood.

What is disturbing about this line of argument is not only the crude manner in which it reaffirms the myth of the Dangerous Black Man, The Black Beast, but the way that it reiterates a racialist logic that stands at the root of this country's many woes. The idea that there are discrete black communities beset by black problems that can and should be solved exclusively by black people is precisely the logic of segregation, no matter how empowered individual black people may feel in the process of its articulation. What connects Clinton and Farrakhan, then, is that neither has yet seen his way clear of the pernicious racialism that increasingly dominates American public life.

Despite my reservations about the ideological underpinnings of the march, it would be untrue to say that I do not understand what drew hundreds of thousands of individuals to Washington on that October day. I went, full of skepticism yes, but also expectant, even hopeful. The first thing that struck me was that it was *not* a march but more of a *happening*. I am accustomed to marches on Washington with thousands of people—singly or in more or less well-organized groups—streaming down Pennsylvania Avenue en route to the Mall. Usually the architects of the mass action try to divvy up the crowd into state-based bodies, collectivities of gender and race, various political and social organizations, groups of students, dignitaries, and so forth. The Million Man March had none of this. The few banners and signs that dotted the crowds were largely homemade, expressing local and specific concerns. Moreover, there were surprisingly few individuals who could be clearly identified as members of the Nation of Islam or even as Muslim. The emphasis was on similarity, the incredible and moving oneness we all shared.

I should acknowledge here how exciting, titillating even, this oneness actually felt. The beauty of the men was startling. It hung in the air like the smoke of incense, intoxicating us all, calling into existence a fantastic vision of community—a glimpse of heaven, indeed. The entire event, not to mention the debates that framed it, was wholly overdetermined by a kind of black-inflected homoeroticism. It seemed that we men could enact millions of tiny instance of love and desire—a touch, a glance, murmurings of "Pardon me brother," "Excuse me sir"—precisely because the women were absent. What remained was a sort of naked masculinity.

A teenaged boy comes up to me. I see his baggy clothes, his corn-rowed hair, the cocky lilt in his walk, before I see him. His face is flushed as if he has just witnessed something beautiful and terrible both, like he has just survived a natural disaster or awakened form some horrible fever. He takes my hand, places his other arm around my shoulder, and says, "All this unity, all this love," presses close to me for an instant, then releases me and keeps moving. I am stunned, caught up in the moment. I imagine that I really have seen this boy, that he has seen me. I am no longer afraid but, on the contrary, rather giddy, glad to be here, to have been part of all this.

At Union Station, I buy a disposable camera and begin taking snapshots of other anomalies in the crowd: women, the elaborately dressed, the not-black. In looking back over these pictures, now as then, I think that there is something incredibly satisfying about seeing reflected, if only for a brief while and through a deeply flawed lens, an image of an equitable, just, and peaceful community. It felt like freedom, a new beginning. Indeed, for a moment, I felt that I had regained that which was lost, had seen beyond the horizon.

Still, as Paul Gilroy has suggested, it is unsettling that the notion of (black) freedom seems so inevitably dependent on polarities of sex and gender and is so often accompanied by a certain desperate insistence on black sexual potency. It seems that the idea of freedom has been so overwritten by fantasies of race and gender that it has become nearly impossible to imagine it without reference to those same fantasies. "The Black Man," as the rhetoric of both the right and the left would have it, is the most *unfree* of American citizens. As huge numbers of black men in this country languish in prisons or under the stewardship of assorted probation and parole boards; as black men continue to be over represented in the drug trade and among the legions of persons with chronic illnesses—H.I.V., cancer, heart disease, alcoholism, depression—as we give our lives over to violence or to a certain silent despair, we have become the very emblems of the ugliness, the bestiality, the barbarism by which the rest of America, particularly white America, can view itself as liberal and free. The image in my mind now is of Rodney King's beating: the endless blows, the irrationality of the white policemen's rage as they labored to drive this black beast even deeper into their collective unconscious. It is possible to chart the past several decades of American cultural and political life by lining up our black male martyrs, criminals, and infamous celebrities: King, Malcolm, Medgar Evers, Louis Farrakhan, Clarence Thomas, Mike Tyson, Willie Horton, Yusef Hawkins, O. J. Simpson, Abner Louima. The list grows continually.

If freedom were truly the ultimate goal of the march, then it was freedom of a discrete, limited kind: freedom from the crushing burden of images—the criminal, the addict, the vengeful lover, the victim, the invalid. Instead, we were presented with an ocean of men, orderly, directed, clean-cut, and remarkably eloquent. Even in their silences. At the march, in the act of rethinking and reenacting our disparate identities, we felt an intimation of some larger notion.

Here, then, despite the regressive racial and gender politics that framed the Million Man March, there were countless improvisational moments of transcendence. The reality of all public spectacles is that the outcome is never certain; no one can confidently predict what its attendees will take away from it, what meanings its many participants will attribute to it. The sad part is that the march organizers evinced so little respect for this wondrously messy and ambiguous process. Once again we were urged to mount the tired horse of black patriarchy. Ministers Farrakhan and Chavis worked to yoke the energy of the event to a simplistic—and segregationist—racial ideology. I still yearn, then, for a vision of the good, for a public dialogue and a civic life that celebrates multiplicity, that prizes ambiguity, that recognizes the play of identity and difference that makes possible community as well as change.

When I die,
my angels,
immaculate
Black diva
drag queens,
all of them
sequined
and seductive,
some of them will come back
to haunt you,
I promise,
honey chil'.
     —"The Tomb of Sorrow"*

The funerals that I remember from my childhood were wonderful, spectacular events. We would give to our dead relatives and friends, and indeed to all the lost members of our community, the pageantry, the glory, the wrenching evocation of love and loss that were most often missing from their lives. My great aunt with her leg severed at the knee, my uncle the stone alcoholic, my grandmother whose breast had been shriveled to an ugly black

* This and all other excerpts from Essex Hemphill's poetry are taken from Essex Hemphill, *Ceremonies: Poetry and Prose* (New York: Plume, 1992).

knot by the cancer that took her life became at the moment of their deaths serene and peaceful, full of joy and hope, the intensely mourned members of a loving family left in this great, if difficult, world. We would lay them out, in caskets of ebony and bronze, wail over their bodies, and then remark with satisfaction that they never looked better. We produced their deaths the way that Samuel Goldwyn produced Hollywood musicals. Unsightly blemishes were cleansed from our memories while our loved ones were consigned to God's bosom, where they would rest throughout eternity. Our loss was heaven's gain.

I am always there
for critical emergencies
graduations,
the middle of the night.

I am the invisible son.
In the family photos
nothing appears out of character.
I smile as I serve my duty.
                    —"Commitments"

He had passed some two days earlier, they told me: ongoing illness, a fall, pneumonia, depression, anger, nothing out of the ordinary really. I was not shocked. I felt no pain, did not cry, did not stretch forth trembling hands unto a distant god, asking why. I still have not gotten furious, cursed the world, fantasized for even a moment about weapons, armies, some great and purifying revolution. No, that would be too easy, and Essex was not easy. At the funeral, his mother testified to his having given himself over to Christ a month before his death. He humbled himself, she reported with joy, before his savior, *the* savior, in the very church

177

where his funeral was held. The minister remembered him as a good son and family member, then warned against the dangers of alternative lifestyles. The friends who told me this were horrified. I listened to their stories, missing many of the details. Instead, I registered the anguish, tried to capture in my memory the odd quality in their voices as they shouted out disbelief that Essex, our Essex, could so easily be taken from us and buried by the very silence that he struggled against so fiercely.

To those of us who knew him, touched him, struggled and cared for and with him, he was a giant, a great poet, performer, activist, and friend. He was indeed the very center not only of an emergent black gay culture but also and importantly the center of everything that was right—and righteous—in this country. He was the personification of our hope and pride. And yet he was a man, one who liked to laugh, to talk loud Negro talk, to smoke reefer, drink whiskey, and fuck. And yes, he died like a man with great strength and nobility but also with marked fear and pain. He pulled back as his health began to fail, giving access to only a handful of friends, making it more convenient for others to overlook the reality of his illness and imminent death.

> *Dearly Beloved*
> *my flesh like all flesh*
> *will be served*
> *at the feast of worms.*
> *I am looking for signs of God*
> *as I sodomize my prayers.*
> *—"Heavy Breathing"*

I have begun saying to those who will listen that with Essex gone my childhood comes to an end. There is no one in my life who captures that regal, almost breathtaking quality that was Essex's. There is no one whom I approach with the same odd combination of familiarity and respect, with whom I always feel somewhat nervous even as I am enveloped in acceptance and love. Indeed Essex was among the last of the living black gay men who helped more than a decade ago to initiate me into a life of homosex, intellectualism, and cultural activism. I have long since taken to repeating the names of my brothers who have gone before me like a mantra, anxious words thrown against the darkness: Joseph Beam, Ray Melrose, David Frechette, Rory Buchanan, Donald Woods, Roy Gonsalves, Assotto Saint, Marlon Riggs; the list continues. I needed them so deeply. My lust for their flesh, their intellects, their spirits was so immaculate, so wonderfully new, almost surreal. And yet it seems that always they pass away from me just as I recognize that they are not gods but men, beings whose fallibility and mortality are the very things that bring them within my grasp, that allow both intimacy and love.

Occasionally I long
to fuck a dead man
I never slept with.
I pump up my temperature
imagining his touch
as I stroke my wishbone,
wanting to raise him up alive,
wanting my fallen seed
to produce him full-grown
and breathing heavy
when it shoots across my chest;
wanting him upon me,
alive and aggressive,

> *intent on his sweet buggery*
> *even if my eyes do*
> *lack a trace of blue.*
> > —*"Heavy Breathing"*

And us? And now? There are those who will tell you that our communities and our struggles have been irrevocably debilitated by all this death, that with so many warriors gone we have become demoralized, battle weary, and ready to surrender. And yet we remain so wonderfully vibrant and, dare I say, alive. Strangely, then, we have become masters of death and dying, turning human anguish and tragedy into remarkably beautiful, if heavy-handed, drama. The culture industry loves the story of the good homosexual come to a bad end. My friends, on the other hand, are all well-employed, many servicing the machines built around and upon our rotting corpses. We find once again that America loves our pathos and is willing to pay for it.

Will you remember Essex? Remember, then, that he was a nigger and a faggot, one who died tragically of AIDS long before he wanted to go. Remember that he did not simply rail against racism and homophobia as they occurred out there in the never-never land of straight America but within the lesbian and gay community itself, including the black lesbian and gay community. Remember that his death was neither understandable, nor inevitable, but the direct result of willful neglect and abuse. Please light no candles, write no poems, do not erase the hurt. The memory can not replace the man.

> *When my brother fell*
> *I picked up his weapons*
> *and never once questioned*

whether I could carry
the weight and grief,
the responsibility he shouldered.
I never questioned
whether I could aim
or be as precise as he.
He had fallen,
and the passing ceremonies
marking his death
did not stop the war.
　　—"When My Brother Fell"

Notes

Notes to the Introduction

1. Richard Rorty, *Achieving Our Country: Leftist Thought in Twentieth-Century America* (Cambridge, Mass.: Harvard University Press, 1998) 14–15. See also: John Patrick Diggins, *The Rise and Fall of the American Left* (New York: W.W. Norton, 1992); Russell Jacoby, *The Last Intellectuals: American Culture in the Age of Academe* (New York: Basic Books, 1987).

2. Žižek writes:

> *Today, however, the very terrain of the struggle has changed: the post-political liberal establishment not only fully acknowledges the gap between mere formal equality and its actualization/implementation, it not only acknowledges the exclusionary logic of "false" ideological universality; it even actively fights it by applying to it a vast legal-psychological-sociological network of measures, from identifying the specific problems of every group and subgroup (not only homosexuals, but African-American lesbians, African-American lesbian mothers, African-American unemployed lesbian mothers . . .) up to proposing a set of measures ("affirmative action," etc.) to rectify the wrong.*
>
> *What such a tolerant procedure precludes is the gesture of* politicization *proper: although the difficulties of being an African-American unemployed lesbian mother are adequately catalogued right down to its more specific features, the concerned subject none the less somehow "feels" that there is something "wrong" and "frustrating" in this very effort to mete out justice to her specific predicament—what she is deprived of is the possibility of "metaphoric" elevation of her specific "wrong" into a stand-in for the universal "wrong."*

Slavoj Žižek, *The Ticklish Subject: The Absent Centre of Political Ontology* (New York: Verso, 1999) 203–204.

3. The reference is to Mailer's much maligned *White Negro*. See Norman Mailer, *The White Negro* (San Francisco: City Lights, 1957).

Notes to Chapter 1

1. Andrew Hacker, "Jewish Racism, Black Anti-Semitism," *Reconstruction* 1:3 (1991).

2. Henry Louis Gates, Jr., *Figures in Black: Words, Signs and the "Racial" Self* (New York: Oxford University Press, 1987) 25.

3. C. Eric Lincoln, *The Black Muslims in America* (New York: Kayaod Publications, Ltd., 1963) xxiii.

4. Zygmunt Bauman, *Modernity and Ambivalence* (Ithaca, N.Y.: Cornell University Press, 1991).

5. Historical Research Department, Nation of Islam, *The Secret Relationship between Blacks and Jews* (Chicago: Nation of Islam, 1991) vii.

6. Louis Althusser, *Lenin and Philosophy, and Other Essays* (New York: Monthly Review Press, 1971) 174.

7. Stanley Elkins, *Slavery: A Problem in American Institutional and Intellectual Life* (Chicago: University of Chicago Press, 1959).

8. Tony Martin, *The Jewish Onslaught: Despatches from the Wellesley Battlefront* (Dover, Mass.: Majority Press, 1993).

Notes to Chapter 2

1. Ross Posnock, *Color and Culture: Black Writers and the Making of the Modern Intellectual* (Cambridge, Mass.: Harvard University Press, 1998).

2. The reference here is to Paul Gilroy's discussion of ships and sailing in his study of what may be termed black cosmopolitanism. Paul Gilroy, *The Black Atlantic: Modernity and Double Consciousness* (Cambridge, Mass.: Harvard University Press, 1993).

3. Ralph Ellison, "The World and the Jug," in Ralph Ellison, *Shadow and Act* (New York: Vintage Books, 1953) 132.

4. See Anthony Appiah, "The Uncompleted Argument: Du Bois and the Illusion of Race." *Critical Inquiry* 12.1 (Autumn 1985): 21–37.

5. Michael Lind, *The Next American Nation: The New American Nationalism and the Fourth American Revolution* (New York: Free Press, 1996).

6. Wilson Jeremiah Moses, *Afrotopia: The Roots of African American Popular History* (New York: Oxford University Press, 1998).

7. William Ferris, *The African Abroad, or, His Evolution in Western Civilization, Tracing His Development under Caucasian Milieu* (New Haven: Tuttle, Morehouse and Taylor Press, 1913).

Notes to Chapter 3

1. Jean Genet, "Introduction to the First Edition," in George Jackson, *Soledad Brother: The Prison Letters of George Jackson* (1970; reprint, Chicago: Lawrence Hill Books, 1994) 332.

2. George Jackson, *Soledad Brother: The Prison Letters of George Jackson* (1970; reprint, Chicago: Lawrence Hill Books, 1994) 223–224.

3. Jackson, *Soledad Brother,* 287.

4. Charlotte Pierce-Baker, *Surviving the Silence: Black Women's Stories of Rape* (New York: W. W. Norton, 1998) 63–64.

5. Angela Davis, "The Black Woman's Role in the Community of Slaves," *Black Scholar* 3.4 (December 1971): 2–15.

6. Frantz Fanon, *Black Skin White Masks* (1952; reprint, New York: Grove Press, 1967) 42.

7. Doris Sommer, *Foundational Fictions: The National Romances of Latin America* (Berkeley: University of California Press, 1991); Nicolas Shumway, *The Invention of Argentina* (Berkeley: University of California Press, 1991); Vera M. Kutzinski, *Sugar's Secrets: Race and the Erotics of Cuban Nationalism* (Charlottesville: University of Virginia Press, 1993).

8. See Robert F. Reid-Pharr, *Conjugal Union: The Body, the House, and the Black American* (New York: Oxford University Press, 1999).

9. Malcolm X, *The Autobiography of Malcolm X* (New York: Ballantine Books, 1964) 1.

10. A very interesting exception is Hilton Als, *The Women* (New York: Farrar, Straus and Giroux, 1996).

11. Frantz Fanon, *The Wretched of the Earth* (1961; reprint, New York: Grove Press, 1963) 61.

12. An interesting side note to this issue is the fact that, before the publication of *The Wretched of the Earth,* Fanon developed a deep interest in the work of Richard Wright and eventually came to think of *Native Son* as one of the world's most inspired modern novels.

Notes to Chapter 4

1. Essex Hemphill, "Now We Think," in Essex Hemphill, *Ceremonies: Prose and Poetry* (New York: Plume, 1992) 155.

2. William Wells Brown, *Clotel, or The President's Daughter* (1853; reprint, New York: University Books, 1969); Wallace Thurman, *Infants of the Spring* (1932; reprint, Boston: Northeastern University Press, 1992).

3. Michael J. Smith, ed., *Black Men/White Men* (San Francisco: Gay Sunshine Press, 1983).

4. David R. Roediger, *The Wages of Whiteness: Race and the Making of the American Working Class* (New York: Verso, 1991); Alexander Saxton, *The Rise and Fall of the White Republic: Class Politics and Mass Culture in Nineteenth-Century America* (New York: Verso, 1990); Richard Dyer, "White," *Screen* 29:4 (1988): 44–64; Toni Morrison, *Playing in the Dark: Whiteness and the Literary Imagination* (Cambridge, Mass.: Harvard University Press, 1992); Eric Lott, *Love and Theft: Blackface Minstrelsy and the American Working Class* (New York: Oxford University Press, 1993).

5. I completed this essay some time before the publication of the rather remarkable collection of new essays on James Baldwin, *James Baldwin Now,* edited by Dwight McBride. It was both stunning and encouraging to find this contribution to Baldwin scholarship and in particular the piece written by Marlon Ross, "White Fantasies of Desire: Baldwin and the Racial Identities of Sexuality," which treats in a much more developed manner some of the themes that I deal with here. On one level I am glad to have come to Ross's essay as late as I did, as I am not certain that, had I known of it before, I would have felt the same need to complete either this piece or the one that follows, "Tearing the Goat's Flesh," both of which are in part attempts to offer readings of Baldwin's corpus that do not distinguish a gay Baldwin from a black Baldwin. See: Dwight McBride, *James Baldwin Now* (New York: New York University Press, 1999).

6. James Baldwin, "Here Be Dragons." in James Baldwin, *The Price of the Ticket: Collected Non-Fiction, 1948–1985* (New York: St. Martin's, 1985) 678.

7. James Baldwin, *Another Country* (New York: Vintage, 1960) 430.

Notes to Chapter 5

1. See: Henry Louis Gates, *Figures in Black: Words, Sign and the "Racial" Self* (New York: Oxford University Press, 1987); Paul Gilroy, *The Black Atlantic: Modernity and Double Consciousness* (Cambridge, Mass.: Harvard University Press, 1993); Orlando Paterson, *Slavery and Social Death* (Cambridge, Mass.: Harvard University Press, 1980).

2. Paul Gilroy, "It's a Family Affair," in Gina Dent, ed., *Black Popular Culture* (Seattle: Bay Press, 1992) 312.

3. Eldridge Cleaver, *Soul on Ice* (New York: Laurel, 1968) 26.

4. See Pat Shipman, *The Evolution of Racism: Human Differences and the Use and Abuse of Science* (New York: Simon and Schuster, 1994).

5. See John D'Emelio and Estelle B. Freedman, *Intimate Matters: A History of Sexuality in America* (New York: Harper and Row, 1988); John D'Emelio, *Sexual Politics, Sexual Communities: The Making of the Homosexual Minority in the United States, 1940–1970* (Chicago: University of Chicago Press, 1983).

6. Piri Thomas, *Down These Mean Streets* (New York: Vintage, 1967) 50.

7. My work has been heavily influenced here by Julia Kristeva's discussion of abjection. She argues that the abject is not the same as the object. The relationship of abject to subject is similar to that of the inside to the out, except that the abject is *not* the subject and *may* hold a contradictory or even confrontational relationship to it. She writes that abjection "lies outside, beyond the set, and does not seem to agree to the latter's rules of the game. And yet, from its place of banishment, the abject does not cease challenging its master." Julia Kristeva, *Powers of Horror: An Essay on Abjection* (New York: Columbia University Press, 1982) 2.

8. James Baldwin, *Giovanni's Room* (New York: Laurel, 1956) 7.

9. See Coco Fusco, "Pan-American Postnationalism: Another World Order," in Gina Dent, ed., *Black Popular Culture* (Seattle: Bay Press, 1992) 279–284.

Notes to Chapter 6

NOTE: "Being Dead" appears in Eve Sedgwick, ed., *Gary in Your Pocket: Stories and Notebooks of Gary Fisher* (Durham, N.C.: Duke University Press, 1996) 69–70.

1. Thomas Jefferson, *Notes on the State of Virginia* (1788; reprint, New York: W. W. Norton, 1954) 138.

2. This phrase is taken from Orlando Patterson's *Slavery and Social Death* (Cambridge, Mass.: Harvard University Press, 1980).

3. Here I build on the work of the growing number of authors who locate the origins of black literature and culture in the earliest efforts by blacks to refute well-developed notions of black *in*humanity within Western philosophy, especially, Kwame Anthony Appiah, *In My Father's House: Africa in the Philosophy of Culture* (New York: Oxford University Press, 1992); Henry Louis Gates, Jr., *Figures in Black: Words, Signs and the "Racial" Self* (New York: Oxford University Press, 1987); Paul Gilroy, *The Black Atlantic: Modernity and Double Consciousness* (Cambridge, Mass.: Harvard University Press, 1993); Ronald Judy, *Disforming the American Canon: African-Arabic Slave Narratives and the Vernacular* (Minneapolis: University of Minnesota Press, 1993). See also my *Conjugal Union: The Body, the House and the Black American* (New York: Oxford University Press, 1999).

4. Hortense Spillers, "Mama's Baby, Papa's Maybe: An American Grammar Book," *Diacritics* 17.2 (1987).

Notes to Chapter 7

1. Combahee River Collective, "The Combahee River Collective Statement," in Barbara Smith, ed., *Home Girls: A Black Feminist Anthology* (New York: Kitchen Table Women of Color Press, 1983) 272.

2. Taken from Cheryl Clarke, "No More Encomiums," in Cheryl Clarke, *Living as a Lesbian* (Ithaca, N.Y.: Firebrand, 1986) 40.

3. Audre Lorde, *Zami: A New Spelling of My Name* (Freedom, Calif.: Crossing Press, 1982) 3.

4. Clarke, "No More Encomiums."

5. Barbara Smith, Foreword to J. R. Roberts, comp., *Black Lesbians* (Tallahassee, Fla.: Naiad Press, 1981) ix.

6. Cheryl Clarke, "How Like a Man," in Clarke, *Living as a Lesbian* 13.

7. Michelle Parkerson, "Refugees" in Michelle Parkerson, *Waiting Rooms* (Washington, D.C.: Common Ground Press, 1993) 4.

8. Cheryl Clarke, "Sexual Preference" in Clarke, *Living as a Lesbian* 68.

9. Clarke, "No More Encomiums."

10. James Baldwin, *Giovanni's Room* (New York: Laurel, 1956) 35.

Notes to Chapter 8

1. See Guy Debord, *The Society of the Spectacle* (New York: Zone Books, 1994) 15.

Index

ABOUT THE AUTHOR

Robert F. Reid-Pharr is associate professor of English at the Johns Hopkins University. He has published widely in both the academic and popular press on matters of race, gender, sexuality, and American culture, and is the author of *Conjugal Union: The Body, the House and the Black American* (Oxford University Press, 1999). In addition to Johns Hopkins, he has taught at the City College of New York, Swarthmore College, the University of Maryland, Humboldt University, and the University of Chicago. He is a graduate of the University of North Carolina at Chapel Hill and Yale University, where he earned his Ph.D. in 1994. He is presently at work on a study of the Black Arts and Black Power Movements, *Once You Go Black*. Reid-Pharr is a native of North Carolina and currently lives in Washington, D.C.